PERFECT STRANGERS

a screenplay

Stephen Poliakoff, born in 1952, was appointed writer in residence at the National Theatre for 1976 and the same year won the *Evening Standard*'s Most Promising Playwright award for *Hitting Town* and *City Sugar*. He has also won a BAFTA award for the Best Single Play for *Caught on a Train* in 1980, the *Evening Standard*'s Best British Film award for *Close My Eyes* in 1992, The Critics' Circle Best Play Award for *Blinded by the Sun* in 1996 and the Prix Italia and the Royal Television Society Best Drama Award for *Shooting the Past*, in 1999. His plays and films include *Clever Soldiers* (1974), *The Carnation Gang* (1974), *Hitting Town* (1975), *City Sugar* (1975), *Heroes* (1975), *Strawberry Fields* (1977), *Stronger than the Sun* (1977), *Shout Across the River* (1978), *American Days* (1979), *The Summer Party* (1980), *Bloody Kids* (1980), *Caught on a Train* (1980), *Favourite Nights* (1981), *Soft Targets* (1982), *Runners* (1983), *Breaking the Silence* (1984), *Coming in to Land* (1987), *Hidden City* (1988), *She's Been Away* (1989), *Playing with Trains* (1989), *Close My Eyes* (1991), *Sienna Red* (1992), *Century* (1994), *Sweet Panic* (1996), *Blinded by the Sun* (1996), *The Tribe* (1997), *Food of Love* (1998), *Talk of the City* (1998), *Remember This* (1999) and *Shooting the Past* (1999).

Methuen Drama

1 3 5 7 9 10 8 6 4 2

First published in Great Britain in 2001 by Methuen Publishing Ltd

Copyright © 2001 by Stephen Poliakoff

Photographs © Sarah Ainslie

Stephen Poliakoff has asserted his rights under the Copyright, Designs
and Patents Act, 1988, to be identified as the author of this work

A CIP catalogue record for this book is available from the British Library

ISBN 0 413 76430 3

Typeset by SX Composing DTP, Rayleigh, Essex

PERFECT STRANGERS

Stephen Poliakoff

Methuen Drama

Perfect Strangers was produced by Talkback Productions Ltd for BBC Television and was first screened in May 2001 by BBC2. The cast was as follows:

Daniel	Matthew Macfadyen
Rebecca	Claire Skinner
Raymond	Michael Gambon
Alice	Lindsay Duncan
Charles	Toby Stephens
Esther	Jill Baker
Stephen	Anton Lesser
Irving	Timothy Spall
Richard	J. J. Feild
Poppy	Kelly Hunter
Violet	Muriel Pavlow
Edith	Kathleen Byron
Peter	Tony Maudsley
Sidney	Michael Culkin
Grace	Sheila Burrell
Grace (17/23 yrs.)	Miranda Raison
Sibling's Mother	Anita Carey
Poppy's Assistant	Jamie Bradley
Martina	Camilla Power
Ernest	Peter Howell
Minty	Ellen Sheean
Small Man	Richard Tate
Nazik	Marianne Borgo
Young Waiter	Simon Quarterman
Little Girl	Rosie Stoneham
Mr Degazi	Orlando Vitorini
Young Edith	Emma Sackville
Young Violet	Rebecca Tarry
Desk Clerk	Hugh Sachs
Strange Woman	Natasha Alexander

Nurse	Anna Mottram
Uncle Bill	Paul Alexander
Stephen's German Boy	Yannik Vetter
Doctor	Anthony Green
Officious Woman	Diana Payan
Henrietta (25 yrs.)	Sarah Guyler
Lionel (Raymond's Father)	Jay Simon
Angry House Owner	Clive Mendus
German Priest	Dan Van Husen
German School Teacher	Stephan Grothgar
Stephen's Mother (9 yrs.)	Naomi Muller
Stephen's Mother (18 yrs.)	Polly York
Maurice	Paul Leonard
Ruth	Thea Bennett
Rebecca (4 yrs.)	Courtney Bolden
Richard (8 yrs.)	Ben Heffer
Charles (10 yrs.)	Mitchell Finlay
Old Lionel	Alan Haines
Old Henrietta	Iris Russell
Woman in fur coat	Beverley Walding
Young Daniel	Daniel Williams

Director Stephen Poliakoff
Producer John Chapman
Director of Photography Cinders Forshaw
Editor Paul Tothill
Production Designer Lawrence Dorman
Line Producer Helen Flint
Music Adrian Johnston

PERFECT STRANGERS

Part One

INT. HOTEL BALLROOM. EVENING

A young man in his twenties, DANIEL, *is staring at us in close-up. He is looking decidedly anxious.*

We hear a voice booming over a microphone and some nervous laughter in response. We see DANIEL *take a step back into the shadows, as the edgy nervous laughter spreads.*

Then we see, strictly from his POV, a banquet in full flow, in a large hotel ballroom, but this is glimpsed through a crack in the ballroom door, which is only just ajar. DANIEL *is watching from just outside.*

In the far distance a middle-aged man in his late fifties is moving on stage with a microphone. This is RAYMOND, *who has a raffish, charismatic, rather anarchic appearance, though he is dressed in a dinner jacket. He is in full flow addressing the banquet, seemingly rather drunk, but not yet out of control, his manner is witty, volatile.*

RAYMOND (*responding to the edgy laughter*): I'm glad you like that one . . . it's a long time since I've told a joke in public. (*He grins.*) The bad news is I might develop a taste for it . . . there could be a few more from where that came from.

DANIEL closes the ballroom door almost totally, so that just a tiny sliver is visible.

He murmurs under his breath.

DANIEL: That's enough. OK . . . OK! Quit while you're ahead.

He turns to see he is being watched by three hotel flunkeys; they are staring at him impassively.

DANIEL (*he grins at them*): Just trying to survive this next bit . . .

He can hear RAYMOND's voice through the almost closed door, but he cannot make out the words.

In the distance, across the ante-room, a phalanx of

3

WAITERS *are coming carrying silver plates of petits fours and jugs of coffee. They move past* DANIEL, *pushing open the door, so we get our first full view of the ballroom.*

People in evening dress sit at a series of circular tables spread across the ballroom. They are watching with slightly tense expressions as RAYMOND *moves on the stage.*

RAYMOND: Since a lot of you have been asking me, in different ways, it is true – some subtler than others – what the hell I have been up to all these years, I thought I'd answer that question . . .

He pauses for a moment, surveying them all.

But I'm going to do it in my own way, if I may, with a few digressions, a couple of stories, a little nonsense, and yes, another joke or two . . .

DANIEL (*murmuring to himself*): No please . . . no please . . . anything but that.

The WAITERS *have paused in a cluster at the back, waiting for the signal from the* MAÎTRE D' *to spread through the ballroom.* DANIEL *is watching the events on stage through the gaps between the cluster of* WAITERS.

He finds himself standing next to a young WAITER, *about the same age, who glances at him.*

WAITER: Am I in your way? Are you going in sir?

DANIEL: I'm not sure . . . (*The* WAITER *looks at him.*) That is my father up there . . . I thought I might skip this part . . .

WAITER: Right! . . . I know the feeling . . . it's the worst, isn't it? Your parents making speeches.

DANIEL (*watching his father*): Stuff of nightmares . . .

WAITER: Still, he's doing OK, isn't he . . . ?

DANIEL: So far . . . (*He smiles.*) I have a horrible feeling the best is yet to come.

WAITER (*glancing over the banquet*): Is it a wedding then?

DANIEL: No – it's a gathering . . . not sure what you'd call it

4

really . . . a reunion . . . a convention.

Faces at the various tables.

DANIEL: This is *my family*, you see . . . I think.

WAITER *looks at him bemused.*

DANIEL: You know, it's everybody on the family tree . . . who could make it . . . They invited the lot – even us! Everybody is related to everybody else . . . it's one of those. I didn't know most of them before this weekend.

Both the WAITER *and* DANIEL *survey the banquet from the doorway.*

WAITER: Oh yes . . . I've been thinking of doing that . . . tracing my family tree . . . I'm fairly sure at least one of my ancestors might have been pretty interesting, mistress to the French king or something . . .

Once you start apparently, you never know what you are going to turn up . . .

DANIEL *is watching how his father's speech is going down among the diners, the faces staring tensely towards the stage or glancing down at the table, or stealing quick looks towards* DANIEL to see how he is reacting.

WAITER: Found anybody worth it? Anybody you'd cross the street for, if they weren't family?

DANIEL: Good question.

We see various faces at tables, ranging from the plump and boring to the gaunt and rather weird.

And then we settle on a woman in her early thirties, with red hair, who is sitting on the central table.

DANIEL: Yes, I think so . . .

The woman looks up. Her eyes meet DANIEL*'s.*

DANIEL: I so nearly didn't come . . .

The sound of the banquet begins to recede, as we dissolve out of the hotel ballroom and into the quiet suburban streets of Hillingdon.

EXT. SUBURBAN STREETS. DAY.

DANIEL *is walking towards us along tidy summer suburban streets. He is in a crisp suit and tie, and is carrying a small suitcase.*

As we move with him we can hear a voice calling faintly at first. As we turn the corner of the street, the voice grows louder.

From DANIEL*'s POV we see two cars parked in front of a semi-detached thirties house.*

A tall gangling man, UNCLE BILL, *is standing by the second and larger of the two cars, which is squashed full of people. He is calling towards the house. The front door is open.*

UNCLE BILL: Raymond, come on, Raymond! . . .

In the first car, a middle-aged woman is sitting, smartly dressed, in the front seat. This is ESTHER, DANIEL*'s mother. She too is periodically calling out to the house, but in an enraged tone.*

ESTHER: Raymond . . . this is ridiculous! Raymond, come out here at once! . . .

DANIEL pauses for a second surveying the scene, the neat suburban street, with roses in the front gardens, the two cars ready to leave, the neighbours watching, and his mother and UNCLE BILL *baying at the house.*

DANIEL (*as he reaches the car*): Hi, Mum . . . (*He waves at the second car.*) Hi, Uncle Bill . . . I thought if I arrived really late I would have missed all this.

UNCLE BILL: No chance . . .

ESTHER: We were literally all here in the car ready to leave the moment you arrived – and suddenly your father disappears in there. Says he's having second thoughts . . .

UNCLE BILL (*smoking, laconic smile*): I never thought he'd get this far actually.

ESTHER (to DANIEL): Well, I'm not dealing with this. I've

already been in three times. You go and talk to him. You
try to get him out of there . . .

INT. DANIEL'S PARENTS' HOUSE. DAY.
DANIEL *moves through the house into the sitting room.*

*In contrast to the very conventional exterior of the house, the
interior has some startling contemporary furniture, an eclectic
collection of pictures and prints on the wall.*

DANIEL *is confronted by the sight of his father sitting in a deep
armchair, dressed in shirt and jeans.*

As his father catches sight of him he calls out to DANIEL.

RAYMOND: You're not going to tell me you're absolutely
    panting to go too, are you!?

EXT. DANIEL'S PARENTS' HOUSE. DAY.
The convoy of two cars, waiting. UNCLE BILL *is chain-smoking;*
ESTHER, *still in the front seat of the first car, is very conscious of
the neighbours watching – two cars loaded up and going nowhere.*

INT. DANIEL'S PARENTS' HOUSE. DAY.
RAYMOND *is eyeing his son. His manner is obstinate, but
amused.*

RAYMOND: You look ridiculous like that. Why did you get
    yourself all dressed up for them?
DANIEL: Well, one of us had to go looking like this – and I
    knew it wasn't going to be you . . .
    He looks at his father sitting defiantly in the chair.
    Come on, you know you really want to go . . .
RAYMOND *(grins)*: That is certainly not true! None of them

have been near us for years . . . And suddenly this reunion! Why now? Why are they having it . . .? And more to the point why on earth should we go?!

DANIEL: It's two nights in a 'prime West End hotel' free of charge . . . that can't be bad.

RAYMOND: I shouldn't get too excited about that – (*He smiles.*) They'll probably put us in the broom cupboard . . . the whole Hillingdon contingent on a different floor from everybody else, right above the kitchens!

DANIEL: You're *already* winding yourself up – and we haven't even got out of the house!

DANIEL's eyes have been roving over the family photographs during this exchange. The mantelpiece has a cluster of pictures, his parents as a couple, their wedding, DANIEL's face during the different years of his development. And an extraordinary photo, that looks like from the early 1950s, of two small boys staring out from a stone balustrade in the garden of some great house. The balustrade is adorned by griffins and vultures, and each boy has climbed on top of a griffin. But they are staring, transfixed by something behind the camera, something that has them screaming with excitement and laughter.

DANIEL picks up this last photo and we get closer and closer to it as DANIEL stares at it.

DANIEL: I've always wondered what you were laughing at in this picture . . .

He stares at the image of his father as a young boy.

RAYMOND: I have no idea . . . not the foggiest clue what's going on there!

DANIEL (*sharp grin*): Why do you have it on display then?

RAYMOND: I like the stone beasts . . .

DANIEL takes another look at it. The griffins and the boys, a mysterious beautiful picture. He puts it back on the mantelpiece.

RAYMOND (*watching his son*): You really want to spend the whole weekend in central London holed up with a load of elderly relatives, none of whom you've ever met before?!

DANIEL (*turns from the mantelpiece and smiles*): The food should be good, shouldn't it! (*He stares at his father.*) I don't believe you're not a *bit* curious . . .

EXT. RAYMOND'S CAR. DAY.

The two cars journeying out of Hillingdon to central London, UNCLE BILL *driving close behind the first car that contains* RAYMOND, ESTHER *and* DANIEL.

ESTHER (*from the front seat*): Is Uncle Bill behind?

DANIEL (*turns and looks through the rear window*): Yes, he's right there. (*Smiles.*) The Hillingdon contingent is going to arrive absolutely together . . .

UNCLE BILL *is driving with a laconic grin on his face, in a cloud of cigarette smoke, surrounded by his family, crammed into the car.*

DANIEL (*from the back seat*): You've really had no contact with the rest of the family? . . . Any of them? I mean, nothing you haven't told me . . .

RAYMOND: Nope.

DANIEL: There must have been a couple of funerals surely or –

RAYMOND: Nothing, since my dad's memorial service fifteen years ago!

DANIEL: Right . . .

So it *is* weird, isn't it . . .

Why they're having this reunion now?

RAYMOND: I think the old bastard Ernest suddenly got interested in his family and his roots, in genealogy and all that rubbish.

9

ESTHER: He's getting older. . . it's quite natural to want to bring everyone together . . .

RAYMOND: Must be costing him a hell of a lot too! (*He grins.*) That's what you can do when you're that rich . . .

DANIEL: If it's been that long – you'll have a bit of trouble recognising some of them, won't you?

RAYMOND: Maybe . . . but ignorance has a certain charm – at least we won't be expected to know who's had a baby, whose marriage has broken up . . . who's got off with whom . . .

DANIEL: Yes – you're right . . . very few of them will know who I am. Or rather nobody will know what I do – (*Lightly.*) So I could be anything . . . I could pass myself off as something completely different.

DANIEL *watches the suburbs recede.*

RAYMOND: Absolutely . . . (*Glancing around as he drives.*) Most of them probably think Hillingdon is in Scotland . . .

As DANIEL *is staring out of the window, he suddenly sees* Uncle Bill *turn off the dual carriageway and begin to fade from view down the slip road.*

UNCLE BILL *gives them a little wave as he goes, smiling broadly through his cigarette smoke as he disappears back to the suburbs.*

ESTHER (*instinctively calling out*): Bill! . . . What's happened . . . ? Where's he going? . . .

RAYMOND: Wise bugger! Thought better of it. He obviously knows something we don't!

DANIEL *watches* UNCLE BILL*'s car disappear from sight.*

We dissolve from the receding road to the camera moving along the branches of the London Underground map, from the outer reaches around Hillingdon, along the Metropolitan line and in a series of dissolves we move into central London,

along the Piccadilly, Bakerloo and Central lines, never
coming completely to rest.

INT. HOTEL LOBBY. DAY.
A grand, rather beautiful lobby of one of London's great hotels.
Lights glowing, people milling, a sense of central London tourist
grandeur, an Edwardian building, with a touch of Ye Olde
English decor.

But there is just a tinge of shabbiness. In the far corner of the
lobby some redecorating is going on.

RAYMOND, ESTHER *and* DANIEL *come through the doors into*
the lobby at a rapid pace. DANIEL *is carrying a lot of the luggage*
for his parents.

RAYMOND *is looking exasperated, striding quickly towards the*
reception desk, his bustling demeanour contrasting sharply with
the languid ease of the lobby.

A very short DESK CLERK *with a large head and extremely*
superior manner greets him.

RAYMOND: Jesus, even finding a parking space for a few
    minutes is impossible round here! We've been driving
    round and round in circles . . .
DESK CLERK (*supercilious tone*): We can arrange somebody to
    take your car down to our car park, of course, sir . . . I
    just need your name.
RAYMOND: Symon . . . that's with a Y. Yet another Symon –
    Raymond Symon. In fact I'm part of this great family
    gathering they are having here. (*He grins.*) You *are*
    having one here? . . .
DESK CLERK: Oh, very much so, sir.
    As this exchange is taking place, DANIEL *is instinctively*
    holding back a few paces. He is glancing round the foyer. He
    sees a cluster of gorgeous-looking young women glancing

towards him. He looks intrigued, wondering if they could possibly be related.

Across the foyer we see a woman emerge from the lifts, she is in her fifties – this is ALICE. *There is something immediately arresting about her. She moves across the lobby as if she's very accustomed to these surroundings. She approaches two plump* SISTERS, *women in their early seventies, who are waiting on a sofa nervously munching biscuits. They spring up to greet* ALICE *as if she is royalty approaching.* DANIEL *watches all this.* ALICE *is very stylishly dressed, giving her both an authority and subtle glamour. Various other figures are in the foyer, some strange furtive faces, some huge bulbous red-faced men, then* DANIEL*'s gaze returns to the cluster of young women.*

DANIEL (*to* ESTHER): Do you know any of these people? What about those? (*He smiles, indicating the women.*) Do you think *they're* related to us, by any chance . . . ?

ESTHER: Judging by what I've seen of your father's family – I think that's highly unlikely.

The superior DESK CLERK *is checking his lists, scrolling through the computer.*

DESK CLERK: A Mr *Ray*-mond Symon? You just don't seem to be here . . . We've got a Mr Ronald Symon . . . and yes, a Mr Reginald Symon . . . but no *Ray*-mond Symon. No – I don't have you here . . . not on the main list, and no, not even on the supplementary list . . .

RAYMOND (*amused*): Not even on the supplementary list?! Splendid – I can go home then! (*Turns to* DANIEL *and* ESTHER). Come on, you lot, incredible piece of luck – we can go home!

Suddenly the organiser, POPPY, *appears, a woman in her thirties, a bustle of efficiency and energy, swooping into their presence.*

POPPY: It's all right . . . this gentleman here – (*she looks at*

him) – it is Raymond, isn't it? . . . Hi, I'm Poppy, I'm
married to Tony and – never mind, I'll show you how
we all join up in a moment . . . (*Back to the desk clerk.*)
Yes, this gentleman here is on the appendix list, I think
in fact it's labelled 'Assorted Extras' because he was so
late in replying . . .

DESK CLERK (*staring at screen*): Oh, there you are . . . oh yes.
I've found you right down there . . .

INT. HOTEL PASSAGES/OFFICE. DAY
POPPY *leads them down the hotel passages towards the suite of
offices that she has taken over. She is in full flow, talking very
fast.*

POPPY: This will hardly take any time at all – but we like
everybody to do this. (*To* RAYMOND). According to
Stephen – who you're going to see in a little while – we
met when I was a child, you and me, I'm sure neither of
us can remember it. I know I can't! It's funny what you
remember, isn't it – some things stick for ever, and
others leave no impression at all . . .
*They go through the doors into a largish room, full of
computers and masses of paper but the room is dominated by
a large family tree that has been printed on boards and
pinned along one entire stretch of the wall. It breaks off by
the doorway and then snakes round behind you, as you enter
the room. The family tree is pock-marked with mostly large
red drawing pins, with a sprinkling of yellow and blue ones.
These are pushed into the tree next to various names.*
  RAYMOND *whistles as he sees the extent of the family tree,
and* DANIEL *and* ESTHER *stare at it, intrigued, turning
round, trying to take it all in.*
POPPY: We've been here a few days getting everything

organised . . .

RAYMOND: Blimey! . . . I had no idea how far the family
went . . .

POPPY: The red drawing pins indicate those already here, the
yellow ones those that are expected, the blue,
cancellations or refusals – and no drawing pins means
you're dead!

RAYMOND: We have to own up to a cancellation, my brother
Bill, in the end, sadly couldn't make it . . .

POPPY (*to* DANIEL, *who's near the family tree*): In that case, if
you could put a blue one in there please . . .

DANIEL *stands before the expanse of the family tree, staring
up, searching all the branches for* UNCLE BILL *and the
Hillingdon contingent.*

*On the other side of the room a tall Italian-looking man,
with a very smiley appearance, is standing with a young boy
of eighteen who is supervising him.*

POPPY: Are you all right there, Mr Degazi?

MR DEGAZI *beams back.*

POPPY: Mr Degazi is just waiting for his printout . . . there is
a printout for each person, a list of the people who have
requested to meet you . . . We thought, because of the
shortage of time, because it's just the weekend, and so
many people are coming – we thought it was a good
idea! Ernest has cast the net very wide – which is so
exciting, but it has made our job rather difficult . . .

*The printer is disgorging an exceptionally long piece of
paper.*

POPPY (*cheerful*): Goodness, you're popular, Mr Degazi! (*She
turns back to them.*) So here's your schedule, as you see
there's lots going on – there are only a couple of things
that are really a three-line whip, that's the buffet tonight
and the banquet tomorrow.

And oh, of course, Stephen Symon! He's the family

archivist . . . meeting him, as I mentioned. There's a slot
for you at six fifteen today, *please* try to make that, he
puts so much effort into it, as you'll see . . .

So you'll need one of these . . . (*She gives them each a
copy of the family tree.*) They come in two sizes . . . you
can choose – most people prefer the big one.

RAYMOND (*smiles*): The big one will be fine.

POPPY: Because you can pin it up in your room, we've hung
boards in all the rooms especially –

RAYMOND *catches* DANIEL*'s eye and grins.*

POPPY: And of course you'll need plenty of *these.*

She pours out red drawing pins.

We cut to DANIEL, ESTHER *and* RAYMOND *in a line
watching the computer disgorge their printout, the people
who have requested to meet them.* POPPY, *smiling cheerfully,
collects the last one.*

POPPY (*studying the printout*): Oh dear . . . only *one name* on
each of these. Never mind, you were very late in
replying, weren't you? (*She beams.*) We'll improve on
this! . . . .

INT. HOTEL STAIRCASE AND LANDING. DAY.
POPPY *is leading them up the central staircase of the hotel. A*
PORTER *is now carrying most of the luggage.*

POPPY (*in full flow*): So it's just up here . . . (*She turns on the
stairs.*) But there's one tiny weeny problem – Not
everyone who's coming is staying here at the hotel of
course, but a lot are! – So it was not possible to get you
all rooms together – there's *one* room on the main floor
here . . . (*She stops on the landing.*) Down there, where
most of the family are staying . . . The other rooms are
in another part of the hotel entirely. Those *are* smaller.

15

I'm sure you'll want to be together . . . but the big room *is* very, very nice . . . (*to* ESTHER *and* RAYMOND) you may want to take that?

RAYMOND (*without waiting for* ESTHER *to say anything*): You mean, one room is among all the family – and the other is totally away from them? . . . It's no contest, we'll take the one miles away from the family – (*To* ESTHER) won't we?! . . .

ESTHER (*trying to soften this*): Maybe that *is* best, yes. (*To* POPPY.) Let another couple who know the family better have that –

RAYMOND: But Daniel – why don't you take the big room?

DANIEL (*hesitating*): Really . . . ?

> DANIEL *glances down the passage that leads towards the luxury rooms. A glowing corridor.*

RAYMOND (*grins*): Pity to waste it!

DANIEL: OK . . . Sure . . . With pleasure.

> POPPY *and the* PORTER *have been watching this with great surprise.* POPPY *hands* DANIEL *the key.*

POPPY: It's number 36 . . .

> *As* DANIEL *begins to move off with his suitcase, she calls after him.*

POPPY: And you *will* look at the schedule, won't you? (*She turns to* RAYMOND *and* ESTHER.) So it's just a bit of a little walk along here – you'll get an idea how big the hotel is . . .

> DANIEL *looks back, watching his parents disappear.*

INT. HOTEL CORRIDOR. DAY.
We move with DANIEL *along the hotel passage, a slightly serpentine passage, bending round, a sense of exploration.*

A couple of doors are ajar, and DANIEL *can't help glancing through the doors as he moves. In one room he sees a shadowy figure talking to a chambermaid. Another door, a bit further along the passage, is slightly open but closes firmly, just as he gets abreast of it.*

He reaches his room.

INT. DANIEL'S HOTEL ROOM. DAY.

DANIEL *surveys a truly splendid large hotel room.*

We cut to him pinning up his family tree, smiling at the efficiency of the board being provided.

He takes a step back and stares at the tree.

We move along the tramlines of the family tree, DANIEL *in big close-up staring up and down. He locates himself and pushes in a red drawing pin.*

The phone rings.

RAYMOND: Naturally we're in the broom cupboard . . .!

We intercut between DANIEL'S *luxurious room and his parents who are in a small corner room with chintzy decor.*

DANIEL *(sharp grin)*: You wanted it that way . . . You were determined to get put into a small room so you could spend all your time complaining –

RAYMOND: That's right. Absolutely! This is infinitely preferable . . .

ESTHER *is beginning to unpack in the background, her manner quiet, contained.*

RAYMOND: This way we won't get loads of relatives popping in every other moment . . .

Your room's fantastic, is it?

DANIEL: Stunning, yes.

Just as he's on the phone, DANIEL *hears a strange sound from one of the nearby rooms coming through the wall. A loud startling noise, somewhere between a moan and a growl of frustration.*

17

DANIEL *turns in his room, trying to locate the direction it is coming from. The noise stops as suddenly as it had started. Meanwhile,* RAYMOND *is continuing on the phone.*

RAYMOND: And what have you got on your printout . . .? The one name that is panting to see you? . . . The person who can't wait to see me is Ernest's son, would you believe, the son and heir . . . no idea why he'd want to do that . . . who've you got?

DANIEL *flicks open the piece of paper.*

DANIEL: It's . . . just wait a moment – it's Irving . . . Irving Matthew Symon. Do you know who he is?

The noise comes again, intense, a little lower, more prolonged, a disturbing sound. DANIEL *moves round with the phone, trying to pinpoint it.*

DANIEL: Dad, give me your room number, I'll call you back. No, no . . . I've just got to do something . . .

DANIEL *rings off. The noise is still there but intermittent. Deeply curious,* DANIEL *moves to the door of his room. He opens the door and moves out into the passage. Just as he does so the noise stops.*

INT. PASSAGE. DAY.

The long tapering pale red hotel corridor. It is silent. DANIEL *glances up and down the passage and at the doors near his room. As he's doing this, a* WAITER *suddenly approaches with room service. The* WAITER *stops at the room next to his on the left-hand side. The door opens, a red-haired woman in her early thirties is standing there. The woman we saw* DANIEL *look at at the very opening. As the* WAITER *enters, the woman catches* DANIEL's *eye and smiles. She is looking radiant and in a very good mood – unlikely to be the source of the noise.* DANIEL *can see beyond her into the room. A pair of male legs are stretched out on the bed, and we can hear a voice: 'Just put it down there' . . . An arm stretches out after the* WAITER *has done this and gives him a tip.*

While this is happening, the door opens on the right-hand side of DANIEL's *room. A pale flustered face stares out at him, a woman about the same age. Her hair is in disarray. She looks as if she may have been crying.*

STRANGE WOMAN (*her voice sharp and clipped*): Sorry – I thought it might have been for me . . . I was just . . .
    She stops and shuts the door firmly. The red-haired woman, who has stepped aside to let the WAITER *leave, has not seen this. She looks directly at* DANIEL.

REBECCA: I'm Rebecca. Who are you?

DANIEL: I'm Daniel . . . I'm next door . . . (REBECCA *shows no sign of recognition.*) Daniel Symon.

REBECCA: So you *are* family. Great. (*Then as if trying to place him:*) Daniel . . . right, we must work out how exactly we are connected in a moment . . . Have you been 'done' yet – processed by Poppy?!

DANIEL: Just now – yes.

REBECCA: So you've got all your drawing pins then?! (*She smiles.*) I would be lost without my red drawing pins, wouldn't you? I expect we get hit with a hefty fine if we don't pin our family trees up – Poppy probably comes round on a room inspection! –
    DANIEL *laughs at this.*

    We cut down the passage to ALICE, *who is just entering her suite, right at the far end of the long passage.*

    She pauses for a moment, glancing towards REBECCA *and* DANIEL *as they are laughing together in the doorway along the corridor.*

    We cut back to DANIEL *noticing* ALICE, *just as she disappears into her large suite.*

REBECCA (*her manner warm and vivacious*): So what were you doing loitering in the passage?

DANIEL: Oh, I heard something . . . (*He glances towards the strange woman's door.*) A noise . . .

REBECCA: A noise? That's sounds exciting. I love the things you hear in hotels . . . other people's moans of passion –

The male figure calls out from his prone position on the bed.

MALE VOICE: Who are you talking to?

REBECCA: It's Daniel – he's got the room next door. (*To* DANIEL) Come in and meet by brother Charles.

INT. REBECCA'S ROOM. DAY.

DANIEL *is introduced to* CHARLES, *a charismatic-looking, dark-haired man, a couple of years older than* REBECCA. *He is lying on the bed, in a summer suit.*

The room is as spacious as DANIEL's. *Yet with different decor. Each hotel room has a different atmosphere and creates a separate world. The colour in this room is rich and sensual.*

CHARLES *sits up as* DANIEL *reaches the bed.*

DANIEL: Please, I didn't mean to interrupt . . .

CHARLES (*giving him a charming welcoming smile*): There's nothing to interrupt, we're just hanging round until the next compulsory moment on the schedule. I'm a couple of rooms down the passage, but for some reason Rebecca has been given the nicer room –

REBECCA (*breezily*): There's no mystery there – obviously I'm going to get the nicer room.

REBECCA *moves around the room and then perches on the armchair next to the bed.* DANIEL *sits in a chair facing them both.*

REBECCA (*indicating the family tree lying on the side*): You see, ours is scandalously still lying there . . .!

DANIEL *suddenly realises he's with these two extremely*

attractive relatives, close to him in age, who he has never met
before. He watches them, rapt. He feels an intense moment of
empathy. We see, from his POV, REBECCA *moving around*
the room and then on to the chair, a very alive and witty
presence, and CHARLES *confidently stretched out on the bed.*

We see REBECCA *hanging up a coat in the cupboard. For*
a moment she smoothes the vivid red lining, the colour
. *reflecting on her face.* DANIEL *is watching her closely.*

REBECCA (*suddenly*): Daniel . . . . ?

DANIEL *hasn't realised how much he has been staring at*
them.

DANIEL: Sorry . . . I was . . . I was . . .

REBECCA: Thinking how great it is that there are some people
here who are under sixty?! (*She laughs.*) I know that's
what *I'm* thinking.

CHARLES: We keep bumping into spooky, oddly shaped
people who claim to be our relations –

REBECCA: And we haven't the foggiest clue who they are.

CHARLES: It's a bit like one's very first days at university, you
have no idea who you are going to meet, who's on your
staircase.

REBECCA *is looking at* DANIEL, *she seems to catch his*
thoughts as they form.

REBECCA: I feel Daniel maybe thinking, how come we don't
know each other? We're family, we're quite close in age,
and we've never met . . .!

DANIEL: That's right. I mean, I know why we haven't . . .

REBECCA: But it's still weird, isn't it . . .?

DANIEL *is glancing towards* CHARLES *and the book he is*
reading, Christopher Isherwood's Prater Violet.

CHARLES (*catches his glance*): You know this book?

DANIEL: Yes, I do . . . (*He smiles.*) It's funny . . . (*embarrassed*
for a moment, then decides to say it) you might not believe
this, but it's one of my favourites . . .

REBECCA: That's a good start!

(She picks up the family tree.)

So let's have a look where we are, do the ceremonial pinning-up.

She studies the family tree as she pins it up.

DANIEL: I'm Raymond's son. (*He smiles.*) We are the ones that live in remotest Hillingdon. The Symons from Hillingdon.

CHARLES: Black sheep . . . that great phrase. Wasn't somebody the 'black sheep' . . . ? Your grandfather . . . ?

DANIEL: I believe so.

REBECCA (*looking at family tree*): Brothers . . . our grandfathers were brothers . . . mind you, they had an awful lot of brothers and sisters . . . (*She glances from tree to* DANIEL.) So what do you do? Daniel from Hillingdon?

DANIEL: What do I do?

CHARLES: Yes.

DANIEL *hesitates.*

REBECCA: You don't seem very sure . . .? (*She laughs*) Were you in the middle of changing? – Were you going to make something up because no one here knows what you do . . .?

DANIEL (*grins*): It had crossed my mind I might do that . . . (*He pauses.*) I'm a surveyor.

CHARLES (*immediately interested*): Really – a surveyor? . . . A surveyor of property? Truly?

DANIEL (*startled by the reaction*): Yes.

REBECCA: That's really interesting.

DANIEL: I can promise you that's not how most people react! –

REBECCA: Yes, it *is* interesting . . . going into other people's homes, seeing how they live their lives, going into their bedrooms, looking at their photos . . .

The phone rings. REBECCA *moves to answer it.*

REBECCA (*as she does so*): Come on, Charles, we must crack open the mini bar for Daniel. (*She turns to* DANIEL.) It's for you.

DANIEL: Me? How did anybody know I was here?

CHARLES (*from the bed*): There are probably video cameras in every room – Ernest is sitting somewhere, watching hundreds of screens, zooming in when he feels like it . . .
DANIEL *takes the phone. He hears a seedy-sounding male voice.*

MALE VOICE: Daniel Symon?

DANIEL: Yes . . .

MALE VOICE: This is Irving Symon. I would like to meet you.

DANIEL: Irving Symon? But we *are* going to meet, at six forty-five. You're on the printout –

IRVING'S VOICE: But why do we need to wait till then?

DANIEL (*covering phone, glancing at the other two*): It's Irving Symon . . .

REBECCA (*rolling her eyes*): Don't let him try to sell you anything.

DANIEL (*back into phone*): It's just I've got an appointment with Stephen at six fifteen, I promised to be there.

IRVING'S VOICE: Oh, it'll be over by then, take ten minutes at the most.

REBECCA: You can't miss Stephen – Poppy would never forgive you!

IRVING'S VOICE: Fifteen minutes max – then I'll be out of the way! You'll be able to forget all about it . . .

DANIEL (*hesitates*): Where are you?

IRVING'S VOICE: Just go out of the door and you'll see me.
DANIEL *rings off.*

REBECCA: If Irving's asked for you, there's no shaking him off!

INT. PASSAGE DAY.

DANIEL *emerges into the passage from* REBECCA'*s room. About eight doors down, a burly figure is standing waiting for him.*

DANIEL *begins to move towards him.*

IRVING: Hi, Daniel, I'm Irving . . . thought we'd get it all over before it gets dark . . .

INT. IRVING'S HOTEL ROOM. DAY.

IRVING'*s room is rather darkly lit, with pale brown walls. It is full of suitcases piled on the bed, and several more spread around the room. Some women's clothes are hanging up on hangers outside the wardrobe, and some more women's clothes are bulging out of the suitcases.*

IRVING: Come in . . . come in . . . what are you doing over there . . . ?

It's not what it looks like. (*Indicating the women's clothes.*) Just some things I have in transit. They're waiting to be shipped out. (*He grins.*) All I have to do is decide where they are going.

They are samples. (*Touching them, handling them.*) What do you think?

DANIEL: Are you in the fashion business?

IRVING: Among other things . . .

IRVING *takes his jacket off, pours a whisky. He has a big, battered, vivid face.*

IRVING: You'll have a drink?

DANIEL: It's just . . . you know . . . I have this appointment –

IRVING: Oh, the appointment . . .

IRVING *is sitting on the edge of the bed with his glass of whisky taking big gulps and staring at* DANIEL.

DANIEL: Yes, I believe the schedule is quite tight . . . you

24

know, Poppy's schedule.

IRVING, *watching him, taking another big gulp of whisky.*

IRVING: Right . . . ! (*He suddenly stands up, puts his jacket back on.*) Since you have an appointment, since you've got so little time – I think we better take a short cut . . .

DANIEL: A short cut . . . ? Where are we going?!

INT. KITCHENS. DAY

IRVING *is leading* DANIEL *through the back passages of the kitchens,* WAITERS *brushing past them, with afternoon teas, full of meringues and cream.*

IRVING: This is my little short cut . . . don't worry, it will only take two ticks . . .

DANIEL: Wherever we're going – (*he dodges out of the way of some ice-cream sundaes*) I'm not sure I've got time for this . . .

EXT. OUTSIDE THE HOTEL. AFTERNOON

They move along the early-summer streets near the hotel. IRVING*'s stocky figure bustling along in front.* DANIEL *following somewhat reluctantly.*

IRVING: Don't worry . . . it's just round the block . . . Will take twelve minutes max, absolute *max*!

As he moves, IRVING *is talking. He has a compelling confidence that sucks you in and makes you believe everything he says. But there's a distinct edge of something untoward, possibly criminal, about him.*

IRVING: You know, this family once had properties all over London – Oh yes! Prime sites . . .

DANIEL: I didn't know that. I'm very ignorant about family

history. We've been in Hillingdon all this time, we lost
touch –

IRVING: Up to *eleven* properties in the glory days . . . right up
to the early eighties in fact. Everywhere you looked –
property!

I was no part of that. I'm self-made, almost entirely,
for better or worse – mostly for the worst! You're going
to be wondering at what – self-made AS WHAT? . . .
You *were* wondering that, weren't you?! It's a bit of a
meld – (*meaningful look*), you know what I mean by that?
A total meld – this and that – coming together . . . well,
sometimes it comes together . . . other times it's a bloody
nightmare of course! Out-of-control stuff . . . edge-of-
the-cliff number!

(*Sharp grin at* DANIEL.) Any the wiser?

We cut to a few blocks further on. The streets have changed.
DANIEL *is protesting.*

DANIEL: I think it might be better if we did this another time.

IRVING: Rubbish, it's not much further –

(*He resumes his sentence, he's perpetually in mid-flow.*)
People always say, 'That's just like Irving!' . . . 'How like
Irving!' But that can't be true, because I never know
what the future will bring . . . I have absolutely no idea
what will happen next – usually – so how can anything
be like me? . . .

So it you hear anybody say that – if you hear
somebody during the weekend saying, 'That's just like
Irving!' – you look them in the eye and you say, 'You're
talking absolute total bollocks – that's nothing like Irving
at all!'

EXT/INT. IRVING'S DESTINATION. AFTERNOON.

A grubby boarded-up doorway and IRVING *struggling with a large bunch of keys.* DANIEL *stares up at the exterior of the building, a disused and rather forlorn small block of fifties offices, no lights on anywhere. Some of the windows boarded up, some sad lettering missing from the façade.*

IRVING: OK, here we are . . . quick butchers in here and we're through . . .
> DANIEL *is intrigued despite himself.*
> *They go through the door, up a grubby staircase, past some dead seventies office fittings.*

IRVING: So there's no electricity . . . so we've got to be quick, before darkness falls . . .
> *They have arrived on an empty expanse of the first floor.*
> You've got to get cracking, so don't bother with any sort of preamble, just get weaving.

DANIEL: At what?

IRVING: Bloody hell, do I have to spell it out?! *You're* the surveyor and *I've* bought this bloody building! Which could be a bloody disaster, or could be a reasonable investment . . .

    .I've had it surveyed, of course, but all surveyors are liars, all builders, all architects – don't trust any of them. But you're *family*, you would have no reason to lie to me – it's not worth your while . . . so come on, I want your opinion.

DANIEL (*very startled*): That's the reason you wanted to see me . . . ? To do that? . . .

IRVING: Of course . . . what other reason could there possibly be?
> *He moves across the ruined floor.*

IRVING: It's the floor I'm particularly worried about. (*He jumps on the floor to test it.*) I couldn't believe my luck! . . . a surveyor who's my cousin! . . . (*He jumps again, bounces up and down on the floor.*) *What could be*

better! . . . I'll get the truth now . . . And the walls? . . .
These supports, are they OK? Those all important
words, 'Anything structurally wrong?' – *You* are family
and you will tell me . . .!

DANIEL *stands watching the bouncing* IRVING.

INT. GROUND FLOOR OF THE HOTEL/PASSAGES.
EVENING.
DANIEL *approaches across the lobby, through doors, panting
along the labyrinth of passages around* POPPY *the organiser's
office suite. As he passes her office,* POPPY *calls out.*

POPPY: You're late, Daniel . . .

DANIEL *goes through the double doors at the end of the
passage.*

INT. VIEWING ROOM. EVENING.
DANIEL *enters a darkened conference room. The tall gangling
archive man,* STEPHEN, *is standing next to a screen on which a
slide is being projected. The slide is a society studio photo of a
very beautiful young woman in her early twenties, taken in the
late 1940s.*

DANIEL *finds his parents standing at the back in the dark.*

RAYMOND (*hisses*): You're so late – they gave our slot
away . . . We're in disgrace . . . have to wait our turn.
DANIEL: Sorry! I went on a little excursion – it was sort of
unavoidable . . .

DANIEL *looks at the sumptuous slide as he is saying this.
The chairs in the room are arranged in rows facing the
screen. The room at first appears quite empty. But then in
the darkness we can see three elderly ladies sitting in a tight*

28

*row together. There are two rosy-cheeked women in their
early seventies, clearly sisters, with bland smiley faces, and a
third very gaunt-looking woman in her late seventies, who is
staring intently at the picture of the young woman on the
screen.*

RAYMOND (*whispering loudly at the back*): I wanted to skip the
whole thing, thought we had the ideal excuse.

ESTHER: But your mother was rather keen to stay.

The tall gangling Stephen calls out.

STEPHEN: We haven't finished yet! Perhaps you could wait
outside . . . Especially if you are going to talk . . .

*One of the rosy-faced sisters, Violet, turns in her chair and
calls out.*

VIOLET: No, no, it's quite all right, we don't mind at all . . .
please talk if you want . . . (*She peers at them in the dark.*)
It's Raymond, isn't it? . . . It's been years, hasn't it!

RAYMOND *acknowledges her politely, not wishing to cause
any further commotion.*

STEPHEN: Well, there are only a few more . . . so we will
proceed . . .

STEPHEN *has a high voice, and a very affected, rather
formal manner. He indicates the next slide. A very prim and
proper woman in her fifties, his assistant, is changing the
slides.*

*Further pictures come up of society portraits as taken in a
photographer's studio in the late 1940s. They are of two
girls, aged about 14 and 16, in evening dress looking rather
ridiculously overdressed, both wearing tiaras. They stare out
with solemn, almost pious expressions, as they stand against
an inappropriate painted backdrop.*

The second sister, EDITH, leans forward.

EDITH: There we are! Do you remember that studio? . . . It
was such a business, wasn't it! . . .

We see them gazing at themselves and we also see DANIEL

staring at the rather stilted and charmingly serious idea of society beauty at the time.

VIOLET (*twisting round to look at them again*): Do you want a chocolate? . . . We have absolutely loads here . . .

The sisters make an incongruous image, with a big box of chocolates as if they are at a matinée at the cinema, making an outing of it.

DANIEL *glances from the girls portrayed in the slides, wearing the dresses that are too big for them, to the plump sisters' faces. He sees they are staring with glinty rapt fascination. But the gaunt elder woman is staring with a very different expression, very severe and intense, her mouth moving rhythmically, almost as if she's chewing gum.*

We move in closer on the two rosy-cheeked sisters and then we close in on the slide, on a detail which lies beyond the two girls standing in front of the painted backdrop. Just visible in the half-shadow is a peculiar detail – two hobnail boots, as worn by hoboes, standing in the corner. We see VIOLET *and* EDITH *exchange a knowing glance, a secretive smile between them.*

The lights come up and Violet bustles their things together.

VIOLET: Thank you, Stephen, thank you so much for that. That really was extremely interesting . . . We're so very grateful . . . aren't we, Edith?

EDITH *bobs a smile.*

VIOLET: And I'm sure Grace is too.

She indicates the older woman who still has a severe unyielding expression. GRACE *sits silently in her seat.*

VIOLET: See you all later . . . it will be lovely to catch up . . .

We watch the three women move off together, the tall gaunt one in the middle, almost being propped up by the other two. A haunting image of three old ladies moving together. There is something about the image that registers with DANIEL.

INT. ALICE'S SUITE. EVENING.

ALICE *is sitting in her suite having tea. A chambermaid is arranging some flowers in a vase. There are a lot of flowers spread around the room in various bowls and vases.*

ALICE: That's fine, thank you – it just needed a bigger vase.

CHAMBERMAID (*glancing at the other vases*): You have so many flowers . . .

ALICE (*following her gaze*): Well, that's what happens, it seems, when you haven't seen people for a long time. It's a bit of a shock though – it's a bit like being in hospital, isn't it?!

CHAMBERMAID (*glancing at the family tree on the wall*): We've had quite a lot of these recently, people hiring whole floors, family conventions, doing their family tree . . . A lot of Americans coming over for it . . .

ALICE: We've come to the right hotel then.

She is stretching to look at some of the labels on the flowers.

ALICE: The odd thing is, the more beautiful the flowers, the more remote the cousins.

We see her reading the labels.

ALICE: It's a constant surprise who's sent me flowers.

INT. VIEWING ROOM. EVENING.

We cut back to STEPHEN *in full flow, his arms making jerking movements, his manner rather comic and over-emphatic.*

RAYMOND, ESTHER *and* DANIEL *are sitting obediently, in a row below his dais, listening to him.*

STEPHEN: As you know, Ernest is disposing of the remaining two family properties in London. And one of the reasons for this weekend is to find out if there is anything in Ernest's possession – pictures or mementoes – other members of the family have not seen, or not seen for a

31

long time which feature them, or would be of interest to them. Is that clear?

RAYMOND: Oh yes!

STEPHEN: And since I have taken on the role of family archivist for one reason or another, it's fallen on me . . . (*his arms jerk out*) I am 'Archive Man' ! . . . So that is why I am up here, so to speak, and you're down there . . .

He peers at them.

STEPHEN: I must say straight away, for obvious reasons, I have a rather pitiful amount for you, Raymond. Your father's lack of contact after a certain point has made this, or rather will make this, a pretty quick showing . . .!

As STEPHEN *is saying this, we intercut between* DANIEL *and* RAYMOND *exchanging amused glances at his manner and the long bony fingers of the projectionist feeling the slides, waiting to show the exhibits.*

STEPHEN *claps his hands together with startling emphasis.* BUT, there is a big but here, I'm doing a talk tomorrow afternoon on 'Dos and Don'ts' for people who want to pursue their pedigree, that is the word we enthusiasts use for tracing one's family tree. So I'm doing Dos and Don'ts for pedigree hunters . . . (*he looks at* ESTHER *who is watching him intently*) aimed particularly at those who have married into the family – because obviously I don't have much for them . . .

He stops, turns the lights off, indicates to the projectionist.

STEPHEN: So – what *do* I have for you?

The bony fingers click the first slide.

STEPHEN: So here's a little sequence I have for you, Raymond . . .

The first picture is the one of the young boys staring through the stone beasts, laughing among the griffins at something unseen. The picture from RAYMOND*'s mantelpiece.*

RAYMOND: Seen this, seen this one!

STEPHEN (*indicating the boy on the left*): This is you, Raymond . . .

RAYMOND: We have this picture . . .

DANIEL: But maybe he's got what you're looking at. (*To* STEPHEN.) Have you got what they're looking at . . . ? That would be exciting . . . I've always been interested in that, wanted to see it . . .

STEPHEN: We may indeed have what they are looking at . . .

The next slide appears of a tall man in a tweed jacket, normal 1940s clothes, dressed as if he is attending a weekend country-house party. But he is caught in a ridiculous position, as if dancing like a sprite on the lawn, with an absurd Peter Pan hat on his head, his legs kicking at a bizarre angle. A weird, uninhibited outdoor ballet. The combined effect is quite ludicrous.

There are five or six slides of the man in this posture. Each one ridiculous, forming a dance-like sequence.

DANIEL: Who's that?

RAYMOND: (*very startled*) That's your grandfather.

DANIEL: I don't remember him looking like that . . . I can't remember him much at all . . . but I'm sure he didn't look like that!

RAYMOND: No, he definitely didn't look like that, I can't remember him *ever* being like that . . . I don't think we can possibly be looking at him in the other photo because I would never have forgotten that –

We see another slide of the GRANDFATHER *standing with the young* RAYMOND *by his side.*

RAYMOND: I still can't remember it!

ESTHER: He certainly never looked like that when I saw him . . . he was always grumpy.

RAYMOND: I can remember those gardens . . . but it must be the least typical picture ever taken of him.

RAYMOND *is clearly very surprised and fascinated to see his dancing father.*

ESTHER: (*quietly staring at the picture*) You see he was dancing for you . . .

RAYMOND *stares back at the picture, not convinced.*

STEPHEN *has been watching this without comment.*

STEPHEN: And you, Daniel, I'm sorry we haven't had a proper introduction. For you, Daniel, I'm afraid there's just one solitary picture . . .

This beautiful image appears of a young boy of about six dressed in lavish period clothes, studded with pearls, and wearing a small bejewelled dagger round his waist. He is standing in a rather ornate setting in some part of a period house, by a fireplace or a recess in the room. It is a full-length picture and he looks like a little prince.

DANIEL: Who's that?

STEPHEN: It is you.

DANIEL: Is it me?!

RAYMOND: Yes, but God only knows where you are?

ESTHER: Must be some party you went to . . . but I have no memory of taking you looking like that to any party, ever.

RAYMOND: Nope, nor me. (*Grins at* STEPHEN.) You've drawn a hundred per cent blank with us!

DANIEL (*staring at the slide*): It's a fantastic picture . . . but I never wore anything like that, I never had those clothes . . . I'm sure of it. I wish I could remember where it was . . .

STEPHEN: What's more I think it's incorrectly labelled. It says 'Black Lodge 1970 something'. And a smudge. But I don't think this is Black Lodge, I think it's more likely to be Grosvenor Place . . . One of the really merry problems I keep hitting is the labelling is totally unreliable. (*He claps his hands.*) Hopeless . . .

DANIEL: So we don't know where it is, or why I was there!
    . . . Are you sure it's me?

RAYMOND: Don't be silly –

ESTHER: Those shoes, if I'd ever seen those wonderful shoes,
    I'm sure I would have remembered them.

*For indeed the boy is wearing these immaculate, exquisitely
decorated pointed shoes.*

The slide stares back at DANIEL. *And* DANIEL *exchanges
looks with his younger self. The camera moves close and
closer. The stare from the little boy is haughty and
wonderfully confident, with just a hint of a smile. It fastens
his gaze on* DANIEL *and hooks him completely. When was
he this little boy? He sits transfixed, searching the picture for
clues as the little prince watches him.*

INT. HOTEL LOBBY AND BAR. EVENING.

DANIEL *and his parents move across the foyer, after the darkness
of the slide show. They are deep in thought about what they have
just seen, the normal hotel guests mill around them.*

    RAYMOND *suddenly snaps out of his thoughts.*

RAYMOND: OK! . . . Best to leave all that behind . . . I think!
    Time for the food – for the compulsory buffet?

As RAYMOND *is saying this,* DANIEL *sees in the distance,
across the foyer, the siblings* CHARLES *and* REBECCA *sitting
at a bar.*

DANIEL (*to his parents*): I'll see you at the buffet . . .

*DANIEL moves across the foyer towards the bar, a subjective
shot of him approaching the siblings. The brother and sister
are looking very stylish, they have changed for dinner.*

    REBECCA *is wearing a backless evening dress.*

    Just as DANIEL *reaches her, she swings round on the stool
and greets him with a warm smile.*

35

REBECCA: Hi, Daniel . . . You've done both Irving and Stephen now? How was it?

CHARLES: Did Irving make you a partner in one of his businesses? – usually he takes about eight minutes to make the offer . . .

DANIEL: Irving was . . . weird. But Stephen was interesting, very funny – but great.

REBECCA: Great?! Blimey, Stephen will be thrilled – I'm not sure many people say that . . .

CHARLES: Did he have anything for you?

DANIEL: Oh yes.

CHARLES: And it wasn't you on the beach? . . . He specialises in beach shots usually –

REBECCA: Yes, awful pictures of one as a toddler in the sand, with this huge pot belly sticking out.

DANIEL: No (*grins*), there were no beach shots – not that I saw. There was a fantastic picture of me as a boy . . . it's just I have no memory of it being taken, or how I came to look like that . . .

REBECCA: Be nice to see it. Did you ask him for a copy?

CHARLES: He does a special little trade in copies. He can probably do a postcard if you want –

DANIEL (*grins*): I might just do that . . .

I'm definitely going to do a bit of probing . . .

DANIEL *stares at the siblings, their confident nonchalant presence, their easy glamour.*

REBECCA: So you ready for the buffet, Daniel?

CHARLES: For the ordeal? . . . (*Mock horror.*) You've got to prepare to 'MEET THE FAMILY'.

DANIEL: It'll be as bad as that, will it?! I just feel I ought to change, after crawling around measuring things for Irving – does it show?

CHARLES: So that's what he wanted. He was using your surveying skills.

REBECCA (*reaches out and feels his jacket*): No, you look lovely . . .

DANIEL (*urgently*): I know it says the buffet is not black tie – so I thought it would be OK to look like this, but I've only brought two suits and this is one of them and – (*Suddenly embarrassed*) – I don't know why I'm telling you this! I've got to change –

CHARLES (*lightly*): According to Poppy's schedule you have just three and a half minutes . . . !

INT. DANIEL'S HOTEL ROOM. EVENING.
DANIEL *splashes water on his face in his bathroom. He looks up at himself in the mirror.*

For a moment he sees the confident little prince from the photo staring back at him, as if he is coming out of the mirror.

He leaves the bathroom and reaches into the wardrobe for a change of shirt, and then turns. He sees that an envelope has been slid under the door and is lying there waiting for him.

INT. HOTEL PASSAGE. EVENING.
DANIEL *stands at the door of one of the suites. He knocks. There is silence. He knocks again and he hears* ALICE'*s voice.*

ALICE: Who is it?

DANIEL: It's Daniel . . . Daniel Symon, I got a message . . .

ALICE: Just a moment, I won't be a moment . . .

DANIEL *is standing by the door, straightening his tie, feeling self-conscious.*

Down the passage a door opens and IRVING *comes out of his room, dressed in a vivid jacket, looking like he's just about to take part in a celebrity snooker competitor.* IRVING *calls down the passage.*

37

IRVING: See I told you you had plenty of time . . . ! I'm still
thinking about what you told me – Could be that we may
have a little business to discuss . . .

He waves again and disappears to the lifts.

The door opens and ALICE *is standing there looking very
elegant. She glances at him with a welcoming smile.*

Alice: Thank you very much for coming.

INT. ALICE'S SUITE. EVENING.

DANIEL *moves into the luxurious suite that opens into a whole
succession of rooms, because the door is open to the next-door
suite. So it is almost like a whole interlocking world of its own.*

ALICE: This isn't all for me, that's Ernest's suite through
there . . . All the suites open into each other . . . they do
that, I'm told, so if a sultan comes along with his whole
entourage they never need go out in to the passage to
visit each other and therefore they can avoid getting
bumped off . . . !

DANIEL (*slightly nervous smile*): Right . . .

*The room is full of the scent of all those flowers, they look
rather magical, lit by the small side lights.*

ALICE: I get given all these flowers . . . because I don't think
people feel comfortable giving Ernest flowers . . .

DANIEL *smiles politely.*

ALICE: I see you haven't met him – when you do, you'll
realise what I mean . . .

Their eyes meet.

ALICE: Wondering why you're here?

DANIEL: No . . . well . . . I . . .

ALICE: I just wanted to say hello really, because we've never
met. (*Lightly.*) You look disappointed . . .

DANIEL No, no – that wasn't me looking disappointed!

38

(*Startled and embarrassed.*) No, of course not . . . I'm
delighted to meet you . . .

ALICE: Good. And me you.

*DANIEL stands awkwardly, feeling he is being inspected.
ALICE sits at her dressing table, adjusting her shawl round
her and just putting the finishing touches to her make-up.*

ALICE: You were so fantastically prompt at answering my
note, I hadn't quite finished doing this, so you don't
mind . . . ?

DANIEL: No . . . of course not.

*He glances around. There are various evocative personal
things, that ALICE has obviously brought with her, dotted
around the room, including a photo of herself when young, a
photo of an older woman from the 1940s, a photo of two cats
stretched out and another of three very young children
laughing together, sitting on a large fallen tree and waving at
the camera.*

ALICE (*looking at herself in the mirror*): Please help yourself to
a drink . . . the minibar is open . . . take anything.

DANIEL: I'll just have some . . . I'll have some mineral water
as I'm sure we'll be drinking down there.

ALICE: I'm sure we will.

*There is some intense music, possibly Tallis, playing on her
CD player. ALICE notices him glancing towards the music.*

ALICE: I like to bring my own music, one of the few things I
have with me wherever I go.

*As she sits at the dressing table with the intense music
playing, DANIEL feels there is something else she wants to
say. He glances at the wardrobe, full of expensive exquisite
clothes.*

ALICE: It's been many years since I've seen your parents . . .
your father and I – we don't really –

DANIEL: Yes . . . there's been so little contact –

ALICE: – we don't really know each other . . . and I don't

39

know your mother either, of course . . . You're an only
child, aren't you?

DANIEL: Yes.

All the time DANIEL *is taking in the detail of the room . . .
the flowers . . . the pictures . . . the personal touches.* ALICE
is watching him do this in the mirror.

ALICE: Seen anything interesting yet?

DANIEL: Sorry . . . I'm sorry . . .

ALICE: Don't worry, I'd be curious too.

DANIEL: I can't help it really – because of my training, I'm a
surveyor.

ALICE: So you must like being alone then?

DANIEL: Why?

ALICE: Because it's a very solitary occupation isn't it . . . a
surveyor . . .? Being an only child and then doing that . . .

DANIEL: Well, you do have a lot of control over precisely how
you use your time . . . but yes, it is solitary . . . you can
get lonely . . .

ALICE: So are you ready to meet the family . . . ?

DANIEL (*grins*): People keep saying that, makes it sound like a
threat!

ALICE: It must be a little odd for you, all these people
gathered together who you don't know, but who you are
related to . . .

DANIEL: Yes, it is a bit weird – especially as I seem to have
only met the more eccentric members of the family so
far.

ALICE: Right . . .

DANIEL (*smiles, hastily correcting himself*): Apart from you, of
course . . .

ALICE *turns. The music is playing.*

ALICE: But you've also met Rebecca and Charles, haven't
you?

DANIEL: Yes – and it's extraordinary . . . it's like I've known

40

them, like we've known each other all our lives . . . !

ALICE *is looking at him.*

DANIEL: I can't explain it really. Not yet anyway . . .

ALICE (*turning back to the mirror*): And you've been given a
   family tree and all that business . . . ?

DANIEL: Absolutely, the first thing that happened. (*He sees her
   tree pinned up.*) I'm already immersing myself in it . . .
   trying to make the connections.

ALICE: It can get addictive, I warn you.

DANIEL: I bet.

   *He sees that all over her family tree she has written little
   notes, and various squiggles and exclamation marks.*

ALICE: I'm afraid I have a little crib sheet about people.
   Because *I'm* expected to know, so I have to find a way of
   avoiding saying 'How is Veronica?' – when they've been
   split up for years and had the most acrimonious divorce
   . . . If you keep a close watch on me when I'm down
   there, you'll see if I manage to pull it off.

   We see the tramlines on her family tree and her coded notes.
   DANIEL*'s face very close to it.*

ALICE: I hope that you don't think this is too organised, too
   like an American convention?

DANIEL: No, I like being organised – it gives one a chance to
   find out things . . .

ALICE: Precisely . . . (*She smiles.*) Mind you . . . if I'd been
   totally in charge of the arrangements, it might have been
   a little more fun . . . more of a party . . . (*Lightly.*) I still
   love dancing . . .

   *She stands up. She looks very fetching, elegant. There is
   something both modern and period about her. She is modern
   in her swift intelligent eyes, and the speed of her thoughts,
   but her careful elegance gives her an old-fashioned quality
   too.*

   For a moment she looks at DANIEL *and he senses that*

41

there is something vulnerable about her, as if she's anxious about something. But it passes in moment.

    ALICE *stops the music.*

ALICE: Later on your must tell me a lot more about yourself, Daniel . . . but first I must ask you a little favour.

DANIEL: Of course. What can I do?

ALICE: I just wondered if you could be my escort . . . down to the buffet? . . .

    DANIEL *looks at her among the flowers.*

DANIEL: It would be an honour.

INT. HOTEL LOBBY. EVENING.

ALICE *and* DANIEL *walk towards the door of the reception, across the hotel lobby,* DANIEL *escorting* ALICE.

    Just before they go into the reception, ALICE *stops and glances into one of the large mirrors on the wall in the lobby.*

ALICE (*lightly*): We look OK, don't we?!

DANIEL: Yeah – I think we look great . . .

ALICE (*moving towards the double doors*): So – here is your family . . .

INT. BUFFET. EVENING.

DANIEL *is confronted by a long thin reception room jam-packed with people who are rather formally dressed. Some of the women are wearing a lot of jewellery, signs of conspicuous wealth.*

    The noise is deafening. Because of the shape of the room people are squashed together into an L-shaped formation, as they swarm around the buffet table, which is heaving with luxury food.

    People smile towards ALICE, *conveying her senior place in the family, as co-host of the party, in the way they greet her. Some blanks looks at* DANIEL *as they see him escorting* ALICE.

42

ALICE *immediately begins to radiate, effortlessly becoming the accomplished hostess.* DANIEL *surveys a vivid series of faces, some looking in their direction, some gobbling food.*

ALICE: Remember anybody here . . . ?

DANIEL: Possibly, a couple from my childhood . . . which was the last time I saw anybody from the family. (*He stares at the hallucinatory spread of faces*) . . . A few little twinges . . .

ALICE: Well, stick close to me, hopefully I can be of some use – guide you through it . . .

We cut across the swirling squashed throng to RAYMOND, *to see from his POV his son escorting* ALICE.

RAYMOND: So that's what he's been up to . . .

As RAYMOND *is watching* DANIEL, *a* SMALL MAN *comes up to him.*

SMALL MAN: Raymond, it's been years . . . is everything OK with you?

RAYMOND: Everything's fine.

ESTHER *who is standing next to* RAYMOND *immediately looks alert, anxious at how* RAYMOND *is going to react.*

SMALL MAN *is seemingly not convinced by* RAYMOND*'s reply.*

SMALL MAN: Things? . . . Things? . . .

The SMALL MAN *seems unable to get it out, his hands waving in a generally up-and-down direction.*

RAYMOND: Yes?

SMALL MAN: Things . . . You know . . . On the up . . . ?

RAYMOND: Never been better.

The SMALL MAN *disappears into the throng.* ESTHER *is eager to get* RAYMOND *to relax.*

ESTHER: Take no notice of that . . .

We cut back to DANIEL *and* ALICE, *as people greet* ALICE.

DANIEL: I'd love to make sense of how we all join up –

ALICE: That's asking a lot! Let's make a start here –

Just at this very moment, a big strapping athletic young woman, MARTINA, *comes up and grabs* ALICE *by the arm and sweeps her away.*

MARTINA: I just need to borrow you for one moment, Alice, you have to come and hear this – it's so extraordinary! It's Jeremy – it's unbelievable . . . we haven't seen each other for nearly eight years – but he goes swimming in the same gym as I do – though we've never met there! *(As she disappears in the throng with* ALICE.) And what's more we go to the same dentist . . .!

DANIEL is left alone, faces glancing at him and then away. He sees through a crush of people an insignificant-looking white-haired man with a very vague expression, who is greeting people at the far end of the room.

Suddenly a voice butts in.

VOICE: That's Ernest, if you were wondering who that is . . .

DANIEL: That's Ernest? That's our host?

The voice belongs to SIDNEY, *a fleshy-faced man with shrewd piercing eyes. He is holding a huge plate of food.*

SIDNEY: Yes! Ernest and Alice are our hosts . . . *(shot of the vague old man.)* Not much to look at is he?! – But he's the one who's made all this possible. *(Licks his fingers.)* And the moon-shaped over-grown schoolboy is his son Peter –

PETER, *a large man in his thirties, but with the look of a giant boy, stands behind his father, bobbing a smile at everybody who passes.*

SIDNEY: I'm Sidney . . . don't worry, I know who you are. You're looking distinctly lost.

DANIEL: Yes – well, I've just been parted from my guide . . . so I was wondering –

DANIEL catches a glimpse, through a cluster of people, of the siblings standing together, talking and laughing in the corner

of the room, by the edge of the buffet. SIDNEY *follows*
DANIEL*'s gaze towards* REBECCA *and the food.* REBECCA *is*
looking extremely attractive in her backless dress.

SIDNEY: You were just wondering how to reach the other side
of the room – how to get across there and make a real
pig of yourself . . .! (*Lewd look.*) That's what we're all
wondering!

DANIEL *turns, very startled by* SIDNEY*'s remark.*
We cut back to RAYMOND, *who is helping himself to*
another glass of red wine, as a waiter passes. VIOLET and
EDITH *approach,* GRACE *standing in the shadows behind.*

VIOLET: Raymond, it's so marvellous you're here . . . I'm
always saying, we haven't heard from Raymond . . .

EDITH: Always saying I wonder if everything's all right with
Raymond . . . ? Wasn't there something? . . . I mean . . .
is everything OK?

VIOLET: I'm sure it is, you know life's little ups and downs,
we all have them. Is everything OK *now* – Raymond?

RAYMOND (*anarchic smile*): There have been plenty of *ups*
because as it happens Hillingdon is the happiest place in
Britain. It is true! It is official. There has been a survey
and Hillingdon was absolutely on top.

EDITH: Good lord – Hillingdon? Are you sure?

VIOLET: I think that's one of the most surprising things I have
ever heard!

RAYMOND: Now if you'll excuse me . . . (*He moves and turns*
to ESTHER.) Blimey! Can't they think of anything else to
ask?! . . .

ESTHER: It's all right . . .

RAYMOND (*taking another drink*): It's not all right! I knew we
shouldn't have come . . .

The clusters of people are getting more and more tightly
squashed together. We cut to the organiser POPPY, *turning to*
her young BOY ASSISTANT.

POPPY: We need another room . . .! I was worrying all night
this room would be too small – I KNEW we should have
taken the Eisenhower room! . . .

BOY ASSISTANT: I think it's great . . . everyone being
squashed together . . . Makes it much more lively.

IRVING *and* SIDNEY *are bearing down on* RAYMOND. *They
form a fleshy threatening double act. Both have plates piled
high with food.*

RAYMOND: Irving and Sidney! . . . Still going round together?

SIDNEY: We hardly ever see each other nowadays . . .

IRVING: I've seen your boy, he seems to know what he's
talking about, I may be making him an offer in the next
twenty-four hours . . .

RAYMOND (*surprised*): An offer? What kind of offer?

IRVING: No, under wraps . . . it has to be under wraps at the
moment!

So, is everything fine with you, Raymond? . . . Are
things better now? You should have given me a call . . .

SIDNEY: It's been years, Raymond, hasn't it . . . never been in
touch . . . I heard one or two things though . . .
difficulties?

IRVING: Business problems, you've been experiencing
business problems, have you not? . . . Bit hellish, was it?!
As I said, you should have given me a shout – I would
have loved to have helped –

RAYMOND: Actually the last couple of years have been
fantastic!

IRVING *and* SIDNEY *look startled.*

RAYMOND: I don't know what you've been hearing – but they
have been stupendous, the best years of my life!

ESTHER's *eyes flash.* RAYMOND *takes another glass of wine
from a passing* WAITER. *We can feel him getting more and
more wound up.*

DANIEL *manages to force his way through the crush to*

reach the siblings, REBECCA *and* CHARLES, *who are edged into a corner, next to a superb-looking meringue pudding.*

DANIEL (*warm*): What are you doing skulking in the corner?! You should be mingling –

CHARLES: Ah, but we're right next to the most desirable thing in the room here. (*Helping himself to a spoonful more of the pudding.*) It's the ideal spot . . .

REBECCA: So are you already an authority on everybody here?

The sea of people in front of them.

DANIEL: No, I was about to be . . . (*He sees* ALICE *in the middle of the room.*) Alice was going to be my guide, and my interpreter –

REBECCA (*startled*): Alice?! . . . That was quick work!

CHARLES: But you got separated . . .

DANIEL: Yes. (*Watching the throng.*) It's a living family tree . . . And it just won't keep still. What's more I left my copy – my tree – pinned upstairs –

REBECCA: Ah – but we've got our pocket one with us – Here. (*She produces it.*) You can hold it up . . . and try to make it fit!

REBECCA *holds it close to* DANIEL*'s face so he can see across the top of the piece of paper with all its names to the swirling figures beyond.*

DANIEL: Yes – I would really love to know where Sidney and Irving come from . . .

We see his POV searching, panning backwards and forwards across the people. IRVING *is masked by a crush of people.*

DANIEL (*lightly*): They still keep moving! So Alice – let's do Alice. (*His POV picking out* ALICE.) She is Ernest's sister-in-law.

His POV slides over to find ERNEST, *and then moves on to* PETER.

CHARLES (*lightly*): Doesn't it make you feel great, Daniel, to realise that all these batty-looking people are your flesh and blood?

REBECCA: Oh, come on, Charles, if you stare at any room of people long enough they'll begin to look very strange, suddenly seem all weird and eccentric. I wish it was true! But actually there are some really boring normal people here –

STEPHEN, *the archive man, pushes through them to get to the pudding.*

STEPHEN: Just got to get some pudding . . . I feel it's a bit like I'm on duty the whole time at the moment (*Glances at* DANIEL *with the family tree.*) I'm glad you're hard at it though!

DANIEL: You know once you get started – it's really great fun . . .

STEPHEN (*sternly*): Fun? . . . Sometimes it's more serious than that . . . it's not all fun and games!

STEPHEN *moves off.* DANIEL *and* REBECCA *laugh at his manner.* CHARLES *is staring at the wide selection of faces.*

CHARLES: It's terrible, I know, but I really do feel I have nothing in common with any of them.

At this precise moment a short sharp-featured woman is pushed in the squash right up to them. She has a cold unpleasant manner.

CHARLES (*nonchalant*): But we do have something in common here . . . this is our mother, Daniel.

The SIBLINGS' MOTHER *bobs a cursory nod at* DANIEL.

SIBLINGS' MOTHER: Hello . . . such a squash!

CHARLES *gives her a small awkward peck on the cheek.*

SIBLINGS' MOTHER: Poppy with all her schedules and charts and printouts – And yet she can't hire a big enough room! They must have known how many people were coming – It's a shambles, isn't it?

People are shoving to get the food, and the SIBLINGS'
MOTHER *is pushed along.* DANIEL *is surprised at this
snappy unstylish woman being the mother of the glamorous*
SIBLINGS.

SIBLINGS' MOTHER: I'm just going to get some air . . .

REBECCA (*smiles*): Short and sweet . . . that's our mother . . .
DANIEL *sees his father take another drink.*

DANIEL: I wish I could say the same about my father . . . (*He
whispers under his breath.*) Please don't drink too much
. . . (REBECCA *is following his gaze.*) My father can get
quite merry . . .

REBECCA: That's all right!

DANIEL: It's not so good when he's really merry . . . I would
hate him to . . . (*he is watching his father closely . . .*) to
disrupt things . . .
We cut to RAYMOND *just as* Ernest, *the host, and his son*
PETER *are walking by.*

ERNEST: Raymond? How nice to see you . . . is everything
OK?

RAYMOND: No.

ERNEST (*startled*): Oh?

RAYMOND: Just kidding, everything's fine – everything's
splendid . . .

ERNEST: Very good! You know my son Peter . . .? Well, of
course you know each other . . . When did you last meet,
do you think?

RAYMOND: I'm sure it's been years . . .
ERNEST *moves on,* PETER *stands next to* RAYMOND *with
just a benign smile.* RAYMOND *empties another glass.*

RAYMOND: I believe we're meeting tomorrow? The only
appointment I've got . . .
PETER *just smiles.*

RAYMOND: Is that a yes? . . .
PETER *smiles gently and nods.*

RAYMOND: Great. Looking forward to it . . .

PETER *smiles again and then suddenly points.*

PETER: See over there? That's Henry! (*a shot of a very
ordinary-looking heavily built man.*) I don't expect you
know about Henry! Shall I tell you about Henry? . . . He
walked out on his family four years ago. His wife said
'Supper's on the table.' (*He imitates a high voice.*)
'Supper's ready,' she heard the door close . . . and four
years later he turned up as a doorman outside a
nightclub in Luton. 'Supper's on the table!' and he was
gone . . .!

RAYMOND (*staring, fascinated*): Amazing – just like that!? –
the missing man . . . Sometimes *I* think it would be
marvellous to do that! (*He takes another drink.*)
VANISH . . .

We cut back to DANIEL *watching his father. From his POV
we see* RAYMOND *take another drink. We see* ESTHER *go up
to* RAYMOND *to try and stop him drinking. We see*
RAYMOND*'s hand go up in an abrupt gesture, he just misses
by a whisker sending a whole tray of drinks spinning across
the room.* DANIEL*'s eyes flinch.*

Suddenly REBECCA *is next to* DANIEL,

REBECCA: It'll be OK . . . (*Her voice soft.*)

*They are both watching his father, angry with his mother,
taking another drink.*

REBECCA: I know it's horrible when you feel your parents are
going to make a scene in public . . . (*Gently, quietly.*) But
it *will* be OK.

DANIEL*'s father sits in a corner.* ESTHER *next to him,
talking to him.*

REBECCA: There . . . it's safe now . . .

Her face is very close. DANIEL *looks back at his father, but
when he looks around,* REBECCA *has moved on.*

The fleshy-faced man, SIDNEY, *is next to him helping*

himself to pudding.

SIDNEY (*to* DANIEL, *indicating* REBECCA): If you think you're
the only one . . . you're crazy . . .!
DANIEL *looks at him truly surprised.*

INT. DANIEL'S HOTEL ROOM. NIGHT.
*In a series of dissolves we move between the faces squashed
together at the buffet, the dissolves highlighting different clusters,
and the tramlines of* DANIEL'*s family tree.*

DANIEL *puts in drawing pins where* REBECCA *and* CHARLES
are positioned on the tree . . . and where IRVING *and* SIDNEY *are.*

*The dissolves are brought to an abrupt halt when the phone
rings.*

RAYMOND: Have you got some milk?
DANIEL: What?

> *We intercut between* RAYMOND *and* DANIEL. RAYMOND *is
> standing in his pyjama bottoms in a small bedroom,* ESTHER
> *is lying in the shadows having already gone to bed.* DANIEL
> *is still in his suit.*

RAYMOND: It's a simple enough question . . . you said you
had a fantastic room, no doubt it's fully stocked, bulging
with goodies – so have you got some milk?
DANIEL: Yes, but –
RAYMOND: Good, then you can bring it along. You've got
the posher room, I haven't got a fridge – so you can buzz
over with it . . .
DANIEL: You chose the room! –
RAYMOND: Don't muck around, just bring me some milk! I
want a nice cup of tea –
DANIEL: It's really late, it's after midnight, ring down for
room service.
RAYMOND: Bollocks – it'll take hours, come on, troll along

with the milk, and I mean *now* . . . (*He grins.*) And you
can have some hot chocolate . . .

INT. THE JOURNEY OF THE MILK. NIGHT.
DANIEL *looks exasperated trying to negotiate coming out of his
room without spilling the milk, which he is holding in a little
metal jug.*

*Just as the door of this room closes, he hears the noise again, the
weird growled moan, somewhere between rage and anguish. It is
not quite so loud as before, but still very audible.*

*He swings around in the passage, trying to pinpoint which door
it is coming from. It stops.*

*He pauses for a second, to see if it's going to re-start, and then
sets off down the passage with the milk, not able to go too fast in
case of spilling it.*

Just after he's gone a few paces, the STRANGE WOMAN's *door
opens. She is in her nightdress. She looks around.*

STRANGE WOMAN: Oh, sorry . . . (*She stares at him.*) I
thought it might be something for me . . . (*She shuts the
door.*)
DANIEL *continues down the passage with the milk, feeling a
little ridiculous. He walks past some supercilious* WAITERS
*who are collecting room-service trays. They look at him in
surprise. He brushes past an entourage of Arabs who are just
disappearing into their rooms. He is just feeling relieved that
he has got across the main floor without being spotted by
anybody he knows, when a voice yells 'Daniel!' He turns to
see* REBECCA *and* CHARLES *coming down the passage
behind him.*
REBECCA: Daniel!? Are you doing room service now?
DANIEL: In a way . . . it's just my father – he doesn't want to
wait . . . you know, he's too impatient for room service . . .

CHARLES: Quite right.

> CHARLES *is rattling some keys, he is standing with a large bunch and flicking them in his fingers.*

CHARLES: We're just off actually . . . do you want to come?

DANIEL: Sure! . . . (*And then not wanting to sound too eager.*) I mean, it depends where to . . . I've just got to see my father –

REBECCA: You might find it interesting – we're going to the house at 40 Grosvenor Street.

> DANIEL *can't take his eyes off the rattling keys.*

DANIEL: Forty Grosvenor Street . . . Really? . . . Yes I'd like to go there very much, but why now? It's one o'clock in the morning –

CHARLES: Well, Minty is the one that looks after it because they're trying to sell it . . . and she's here, and she's fussed about whether she'd remembered to set the alarm – and we said we'd go and check for her –

REBECCA: And let Minty go on enjoying herself here – whatever she's up to! . . .

CHARLES: Coming? . . . (*He flicks the keys.*)

DANIEL: Great . . . Yes . . . I just need to get rid of this milk.

INT. RAYMOND'S HOTEL ROOM/PASSAGE. NIGHT.
RAYMOND *opens the door of his hotel room.* DANIEL *presents his father with the jug of milk.*

RAYMOND (*in doorway*): There it is . . .

DANIEL: And this is Rebecca and Charles . . . my cousins . . . *our* cousins –

RAYMOND: Of course – (*Smiles.*) If we've ever met before you were probably babies . . .

> REBECCA *and* CHARLES *smile at him.* RAYMOND *is standing in his dressing gown and pyjamas. His dressing gown is very*

53

loosely tied and he's fiddling with the cord.

RAYMOND: Anyway, why are you standing there?! Come on in . . .

DANIEL: No. (*Hastily.*) We can't . . . See you in the morning –

RAYMOND: Hey! I thought we were having a cup of tea? Or hot chocolate . . . come in all of you, into our palatial room.

ESTHER is quickly putting on a dressing gown in bed, behind RAYMOND's shoulder. But DANIEL is quick to reply before the siblings can accept the invitation.

DANIEL: No, we're just going somewhere – I've already held them up . . . We gotta go . . .

Disappointment momentarily showing in RAYMOND's eyes.

RAYMOND: Too busy for hot chocolate? OK – Off you go! Dance the night away (*Slight grin.*) You never know, I might do the same . . .

EXT. LONDON STREETS AND GARDEN SQUARE. NIGHT.
DANIEL, REBECCA *and* CHARLES *move along the streets.*

CHARLES: 'Minty' . . . . ridiculous, aren't they – the old family names?! There was Ba Ba too . . .

REBECCA: Yeah, and didn't Ernest have a driver called Jugs?! And an old nanny called Bluety?

CHARLES: Yes . . . all the old retainers. There was a Smidger . . .

DANIEL: A Smidger? I don't believe it.

CHARLES: And a Cogga and Peterbin . . .

REBECCA: And SmoothHarry . . .

CHARLES: SmoothHarry . . . sounds good . . . never met him! Wonder who he was . . .

He is flicking through the keys and opening the gate of the garden square.

CHARLES: Short cut . . . quickest way to the house . . .

They move through the garden square at night, with its little
white temple. CHARLES *smiles at* DANIEL *as they move*
along the gravel paths.

CHARLES: If you have the keys – you can get in anywhere . . .

DANIEL *following the siblings across the garden square.* REBECCA
turns and looks back at him. She gives him a warm smile.

REBECCA: Come on – it's not far.

INT. RAYMOND'S HOTEL ROOM. NIGHT.

RAYMOND *is in bed, his eyes wide open, staring upwards.*
ESTHER *is trying to sleep.* RAYMOND *glances at the phone.*

RAYMOND: You know, it's amazing . . . I'm surprised we're
not getting calls *now* – (*Mimics.*) 'Is everything OK . . . ?'
'Are things on the up at last . . . ?' One of those jolly
sisters will probably pop by any moment . . .

ESTHER: Just leave it . . . it's only them making small talk –
it's difficult to know what to say to people when you
haven't seen them for twenty years . . .

RAYMOND: I don't find is difficult, so why should they? What
they really want to say is – 'We heard you were bankrupt
. . . amazed you're still with us in fact . . . not topped
yourself!'

ESTHER (*trying to reassure*): It doesn't matter . . .

RAYMOND: Yes it does. (*He starts to dial.*)

ESTHER: What are you doing?

RAYMOND: I have a terrible craving, which if doesn't get
satisfied really quickly will have enormous consequences
. . . Is that room service . . .? I would like some
scrambled eggs . . . You don't have scrambled eggs?! . . .
It says twenty-four-hour service here . . . no, no I don't
want a club sandwich . . . you do roast chicken – so whý

55

not scrambled eggs?!

Tell me, is there anybody in the kitchen . . . ?! *So*?!
No., no, you don't understand, I *have* to have some
scrambled eggs . . .

EXT. LARGE LONDON HOUSE. NIGHT

CHARLES *goes through the keys, as they stand on the steps of the
large house, which is in the middle of a terrace on one side of the
square.* DANIEL *stares up at the grand but quite shabby exterior.
All the windows are dark, a lot of them with their curtains drawn
or blinds shut.*

CHARLES (*finding the right key*): OK, . . . here we are.

CHARLES *opens the door. The burglar alarm starts bleeping,
beginning its countdown.*

INT. LARGE LONDON HOUSE. NIGHT

*Immediately on the other side of the door is an ugly sixties
partition which has to be unlocked to get you into the main part of
the hall. On the left is a door to a flat.*

CHARLES *is groping in the dark to find the alarm and silence
it.*

A big shiver runs through REBECCA.

REBECCA: Jesus – it's cold . . . so much colder in here than
out there!

Come on, Charles (*as the alarm beeps on*) – Stop that
before it goes off . . .

CHARLES *defuses the alarm.*

CHARLES: Minty's code is very simple . . . 9999! (*He turns.*)
So let's do Alice's flat first . . .

DANIEL (*startled*): Alice's flat . . .?

CHARLES *is flicking through the keys, seeking the right one.*

CHARLES: Yes, when she's in London she lives here.

REBECCA: Except tonight . . .

CHARLES: Because everybody has to be together tonight!

> CHARLES *gets the door to* ALICE*'s flat open.*

DANIEL (*hesitates*): Should we go in there . . .?

CHARLES: Yes, why not?

REBECCA (*turning in the doorway*): We haven't been here for years . . . The whole point is to snoop!

> DANIEL *stands on the edge of the flat, not quite sure whether he should violate the space.*
>
> *It is a neat evocative flat, lined with books and pictures.*
> REBECCA *and* CHARLES *move through the main reception room and the bedroom very purposefully, as if searching.*

DANIEL: Are you looking for anything in particular?

CHARLES: Oh, you know . . . anything that looks intriguing. . . any surprises . . .

REBECCA (*glancing across the shelves*): Daniel's so used to going into other people's places – he doesn't find it as irresistible as the rest of us . . .

CHARLES: So – any trace of lovers, for instance . . . what does she really get up to?

REBECCA: Alice and lovers . . . Yes – that's interesting (*She looks up at* DANIEL.) Don't worry, it's OK – she's a widow . . .

DANIEL (*slight smile*): You mean, she's allowed a lover.

> CHARLES *is glancing across the collection of family photos. He picks one up and then replaces it.*

REBECCA: Daniel doesn't approve . . .

CHARLES: Quite right! . . . We'll stop . . . looks like we've drawn a blank here anyway – let's go to the main event. *We cut to* CHARLES *spinning through the bunch of keys as they stand in front of the partition wall. He gets it open. It is pitch black on the other side.* CHARLES *ventures into the dark.*

CHARLES (*as he does so*): This is all the bit of the house that is
    shut up. (*He flounders in the dark.*) *Come on* – there must
    be a switch here somewhere . . .
    CHARLES *gets the light on.*

    DANIEL *finds himself staring at the main staircase of the
    house. A shabby but beautiful marble and stone eighteenth
    century staircase, surrounded by peeling wallpaper.*

    DANIEL *instantly recognises it as the setting of his
    childhood photograph. This is where he stood looking like a
    little prince.*

DANIEL (*excited, yelling it out*) This is where it was . . .! The
    picture . . . *this* is where I was standing . . .!
    *He walks up the first steps of the staircase . . . the camera
    simultaneously moves up the black-and-white photo.*

    We cut back to DANIEL *standing on the landing staring
    down at* REBECCA *and* CHARLES.

REBECCA (*calling up to him*): You were here before?!
CHARLES (*horror/movie voice*): He's been here BEFORE.
REBECCA: Remember it now . . . ? Remember what was
    happening . . . ?
    DANIEL *takes up the same position and posture as the little
    prince in the photo. The same viewpoint.*

    *We see, in one instant, a grainy dark flashback of
    childrens' heads bobbing on the staircase in the shadows,
    their young voices echoing round the marble and stone wall.
    Then the image goes.*

DANIEL: No – it won't come back . . .

    CHARLES *comes running up the stairs.*

CHARLES: Let's go on . . . you never know we might find
    something – and it might all come back . . .

INT. HOTEL PASSAGES. NIGHT
RAYMOND *is walking along the hotel passages in his dressing*

gown and slippers. He sees two WAITERS *piling plates up in a pantry area.*

RAYMOND: I'm looking for some scrambled eggs . . .
The WAITERS *stare at him blankly.*
RAYMOND: How do I get them at this time of night?
(*Dangerous smile.*) Can you help me?

INT. LARGE LONDON HOUSE, NIGHT.
CHARLES *unlocks the doors of the rooms on the first floor of the large house.*
They move through the floor at a pace. Each door yields up another large room, full of boxes piled high with belongings, ornaments, old books and photos – especially family photos, sprouting out of the tops of boxes, but they're all soiled, stained with dirt, some torn.
The photos stare back at DANIEL *as they move through the succession of rooms, giving him flashes of the family history.*

CHARLES: It's in a dreadful state, isn't it?! – They managed to turn it into something really sad . . .
He moves around the boxes staring at the objects.
CHARLES: There's always something terrible about houses when they're shut up waiting to be disposed of . . . waiting for walls to be knocked down . . . for their insides to be torn out –
REBECCA (*touching the surfaces*): Minty has hardly been dusting it very hard . . .
CHARLES (*unlocking another door*): This was the centre of everything in the family's heyday . . . their great town house . . . when they thought they would be a tremendous power in London life – in political circles, in the arts, that they'd be members of the government . . . a

59

sort of mini Rothschilds. Sometimes they got close . . .
but it never quite happened.

The old stained photographs stare back.

REBECCA: But he's still got loads and loads of money –
Ernest . . . ? Hasn't he?

CHARLES: Oh God, yes! . . . And his second wife brought her
own fortune with her too.

So he's still drowning in money . . . Pots and pots! . . .

He stares at the damp stains on the walls.

CHARLES: It's amazing what squalor really rich people will
tolerate.

REBECCA (*glancing at* DANIEL *warmly*): *Money* . . . you
wouldn't mind some money, would you, Daniel?

DANIEL: Certainly not! (*Smiles.*) I wouldn't mind at all . . .
(*As they move through the grand dusty rooms*) Surveying
properties in Hillingdon and Isleworth is surprisingly
interesting – as you have rightly pointed out. But some
serious money! (*He's staring up at the ornamental ceiling.*)
Some serious, serious money – I wouldn't say no to
that! . . .

CHARLES: Your grandfather had money, didn't he?

DANIEL: He did. Yes. (*Quiet.*) But my dad lost it all . . .

REBECCA *has stopped by a box of old photographs. She
smiles as she glances through them.*

REBECCA: You never know, you might turn out to be Ernest's
bastard son . . . !

She picks up a dusty stained photograph.

REBECCA: Think what Stephen would make of these . . .

DANIEL: Archive man! . . . (*He mimics Stephen.*) 'It's not all
fun and games you know!' (*He jerks his arms.*) 'Far from
it!'

REBECCA: These are all too stained for him though . . . (*She
smiles.*) Wouldn't meet his standards!

It begins to rain, a heavy summer rain. We hear it echoing through the old house. DANIEL *stares at* REBECCA *in her backless evening dress.*

They reach a room dominated by a very large cupboard full of old clothes. REBECCA *and* CHARLES *look through the old clothes in the cupboard, quickly eyeing up and rejecting most of what they find, as if they are looking for something in particular.*

Eventually they pull out a long leather coat.

REBECCA: Do we want this?

CHARLES: No . . .

REBECCA: Are you sure?

CHARLES: Yes!

DANIEL: Great leather coat . . . (*He examines it.*) From the eighties, I should think . . .

CHARLES: You can have it.

DANIEL: No . . . I wouldn't want to do that.

CHARLES: It's all right . . . it's not stealing. I hardly see Ernest wearing it . . .

REBECCA: Put it on . . .

DANIEL puts on the long leather coat. He stands in the middle of the room wearing it. REBECCA *and* CHARLES *stare at him.* REBECCA *touches the coat.*

REBECCA: It really suits you . . .

She sinks to her knees by the bottom of the cupboard. The shadow of the rain playing on her bare back.

Now . . . how about some boots?

There are various different shoes, and indeed some boots in the bottom of the cupboard. DANIEL *is kneeling by* REBECCA *going through the shoes. Suddenly he cries out.*

DANIEL: Jesus! Look . . . look at this!

DANIEL stretches right into the dusty far corner of the cupboard and pulls out of the darkness a tiny shoe. An exquisitely decorated pointed shoe, one of the shoes he wore in the photograph.

DANIEL: It's the shoe I wore in the picture . . . it really is . . . I
    was here . . .
    He holds the shoe up in front of his eyes. REBECCA *is*
    kneeling by him.
REBECCA (*smiling*): You've struck gold.

INT. HOTEL LOBBY. NIGHT.
RAYMOND *is approaching us in his dressing gown and slippers.*
He reaches the reception desk. The same supercilious DESK
CLERK *is watching him closely.*
RAYMOND: Oh, you again . . . you're on twenty-four hours a
    day, are you?
DESK CLERK (*ignoring this*): How can I help you, sir?
RAYMOND: I have a very particular desire – which I'm trying
    to get satisfied . . .
DESK CLERK (*unfazed*): And what might that be, sir?
RAYMOND: I need some scrambled eggs and room service
    doesn't seem to be able to cope with that.
DESK CLERK: If room service can't help you, sir, we may
    have a problem –
    RAYMOND *suddenly sees* ALICE *is standing on the other side*
    of the foyer, glancing at some leaflets.
RAYMOND: Alice?! (ALICE *turns.*) You're here too . . . it's
    nearly two o'clock in the morning!
ALICE (*approaching* RAYMOND): Oh, I never need much sleep
    . . . in the summer I often go for a bit of a walk late at
    night. (*Glancing towards entrance.*) But tonight it's
    raining . . . I was just waiting, just hoping it was going to
    stop.
RAYMOND (*very surprised*): Right . . .
ALICE: And what about you?
RAYMOND: I'm trying to get some scrambled eggs, but
    apparently that's the craziest request they've had in

years . . .

DESK CLERK: A club sandwich, I'm sure that can be arranged
. . . or maybe even a turkey baguette . . .

ALICE (*to* RAYMOND): Shall I try?

RAYMOND: You try? Why not . . . (*He turns to the* DESK
CLERK.) She's going to ask you for some scrambled eggs
– Think carefully before you answer . . .

ALICE (*lightly*): Maybe it would be easier to do it without an
audience, Raymond.

RAYMOND: OK – I'll shove off over there . . . (*He calls as he
goes.*) If possible, really buttery! . . .

RAYMOND *sits on the far side of the foyer and watches*
ALICE *in elegant negotiation at the desk. The rain is*
torrential outside.

ALICE *approaches* . . .

ALICE: They'll be along in a moment . . .

RAYMOND: Just like that . . . Extraordinary . . . ! What's your
secret?

ALICE (*sitting opposite him*): Well, I've stayed here before . . .
once or twice . . . over the years.

RAYMOND (*grins*): And you're not in a dressing-gown. Mind
you, we could be waiting here for hours –

ALICE: It's possible. (*Confident smile.*) We'll see . . .

RAYMOND: Thank you anyway. (*He stares at her.*) Last time I
saw you – you were a young woman . . . lying on a lawn
somewhere, with your shoes off, reading *Punch*.

ALICE: Don't let's put a date to it please!

RAYMOND: I remember I was rather terrified of you . . .

ALICE: So you didn't come up and talk to me? . . . That's why
I can't remember it.

RAYMOND: You're right . . . I didn't dare approach . . .
Today's been full of people from my youth . . .

ALICE (*suddenly*): Is it terrible? This weekend? Do you think
it's a big mistake – ?

63

RAYMOND: Terrible? . . . Of course not! But for me . . . (*He stops.*)

ALICE: Yes?

RAYMOND: You know, people keep asking for news . . . You haven't – but everyone else has.

ALICE: And that's difficult?

RAYMOND (*surprised*): You don't know?

ALICE: No.

We see RAYMOND *doesn't believe her.*

RAYMOND: I had a little business difficulty . . . my father had this furniture business. I'm sure you remember that . . . My rebel father . . . setting it up in Hillingdon of all places. A utopian firm . . . Stylish office furniture for the masses . . . When he died, we had some good offers . . . I refused to sell . . . you *sure* you didn't hear about this, Alice?

ALICE: No . . .

RAYMOND: In the middle of the recession I poured in all the money he'd left me . . . Moreover, I insisted on only having workers over fifty – because of long-term unemployment – in the teeth of all prevailing fashion . . . I was *determined* to make it work.

　　We went bust. We lost everything. They all lost their jobs . . . Some of them were worse off than before – because they'd taken out mortgages again. Some marriages broke up . . .

　　It was purely and simply a disaster.

ALICE: But a defiant one? . . . A gesture against the times?

RAYMOND: Yes –

ALICE: Something your father would have understood.

RAYMOND *is deep in thought after this remark. He is obviously extremely troubled. We see the picture of his father dancing like a pixie on the lawn.*

RAYMOND: Maybe . . .

64

He hears a sound, a hot-food trolley with a large silver bowl is being pushed towards them across the foyer by a waiter. Another WAITER *follows to lay the table.*

RAYMOND: That's amazing! . . . Alice, that is a true achievement . . .

ALICE *smiles as the* WAITER *slides back the lid to reveal a large stainless-steel tureen of scrambled eggs.*

RAYMOND: That is supremely wonderful!

ALICE (*amused*): Thank you . .

The rain is pouring down outside.

RAYMOND: You'll have to call off your walk tonight . . . (*He grins.*)

I love the idea by the way of you stalking the streets at night . . .

You'll have to join me!

INT. LARGE LONDON HOUSE. NIGHT.

CHARLES *pushes open a door, a rather stiff door that needs a kick, at the top of the house. Sound of the rain bucketing down.*

They enter a room full of sixties furniture piled up: orange and gungey greens, and round the walls, propped up, a series of guitars, four old electric guitars and three acoustic.

DANIEL: Blimey! That's a weird thing to find . . .

CHARLES: Isn't it just!

They move across the room. DANIEL *picks up a fistful of old photos. One of them is a strange haunting picture of* ALICE, *peering from the back seat of a car, looking startled and vulnerable.*

CHARLES (*picking up a guitar*): Maybe they had secret jamming sessions up here . . . the family –

REBECCA: Yes . . . (*She laughs.*) Ernest lead guitar, Violet on keyboards . . . and maybe (*she jerks her arms out*)

Stephen on the drums.

CHARLES: Yes . . .(*He plucks the guitar.*) Irving would have to have been the lead singer . . . a sort of Meatloaf!

DANIEL (*joining in*): And Alice could be on the tambourine – (*They look at him.*) You know, very genteel . . .

REBECCA: Yes – (*Gazing round the room.*) Maybe, Daniel, if we burrow around hard enough we'll find another shoe.

CHARLES: Even the whole costume.

DANIEL: You ought to be able to remember, Rebecca . . . did you ever come here for a children's party? We could have been here together! . . . (*He grins.*) Could have played hide and seek up here . . .

REBECCA (*turning*): I don't remember coming here when I was small . . . but if I had you would have been a tiny little boy . . . (*She ruffles his hair, close to him.*) If I'd been eight – you would have only been about four!

DANIEL: I wasn't four . . . judging by the photo I was around six.

REBECCA: Then I was ten. (*Her face closes.*) That's such a difference at that age . . . an ocean . . . I wouldn't have even begun to talk to a six-year-old.
She suddenly gives him a kiss on the cheek. DANIEL *is startled.*

REBECCA (*warm smile*): It's OK. It *is* legal . . .

INT. HOTEL FOYER. NIGHT.

ALICE *and* RAYMOND *are eating the scrambled eggs.* RAYMOND *helps himself to some more, the trolley is sitting next to them.*

ALICE: When you look at the family, Raymond – it's really such an extraordinary mix . . .

RAYMOND: You can say that again!

ALICE: I mean, does it really make sense to try and bring it together?

And of course the Jewish core of the family has been diluted for a long time . . . Several of my husband's siblings married non-Jews like me . . .

RAYMOND: And my father did . . . and I did . . .

ALICE: And as for my husband! – he tried so hard to play the country squire . . .

You should have seen him hunting in his scarlet tunic . . . He was quite portly, so he had to squeeze, really squeeze, and for some reason his tunic seemed to be a brighter shade of scarlet than anybody else's . . . so you could always pick him out even at a great distance . . . (*Fond laugh, remembering.*) My bobbing bright red husband . . .

RAYMOND (*looking up from his plate, nearly finished*): That was fantastic . . . Alice, and so buttery – not fluffy at all . . .

I never thought I'd be eating scrambled eggs with you at two thirty in the morning – you of all people!

ALICE: You seem to think I'm terribly grand and conventional, Raymond –

RAYMOND: No. (*Teasing smile.*) Now I see there's a wild side! (*Finishes his last scrap of egg.*) So . . . We've done that. Now we don't need to do it again for another twenty years.

ALICE (*very startled*): Why do you say that?

RAYMOND: Because it's true. I very much doubt I'll be around the family much after this weekend.

ALICE: So it is that bad? Being here?

RAYMOND: Yes. (*Genuinely.*) It was very nice of you to pretend you knew so little of my problems –

ALICE: I wasn't pretending.

We see he doesn't believe her.

RAYMOND: Please . . . Don't worry, I'm going to get through

tomorrow very calmly, without major mishap. At least, I promise not to break anything.

EXT. WHITEHALL. DAWN.
DANIEL, REBECCA *and* CHARLES, *moving along Whitehall, just as dawn is coming up.* DANIEL *is wearing the long leather coat.*

CHARLES (*to* DANIEL): How about some breakfast?
DANIEL: Breakfast . . . Where? (*Staring at him.*) Here . . . ?
    (*Suddenly.*) You work here, don't you . . . (*Turning in the middle of the road, staring at the buildings.*) In one of these? . . . In the Treasury? . . . the Foreign Office?
REBECCA: Which once?
DANIEL: The Foreign Office . . .
CHARLES: Not bad –
DANIEL: What you do mean, not bad? – I'm either right or I'm not –

INT. FOREIGN OFFICE. DAWN.
They walk along the marble passages of the Foreign Office.

DANIEL: I was right! (*He turns to* REBECCA.) You work here too?
REBECCA: No, no, no . . . I'm buried away in a sleepy stately home outside London, monitoring foreign broadcasts . . .
DANIEL: A spy?! Of course . . . So that's what you are – a spy.
REBECCA: No, no . . . If only . . .!

INT. CHARLES'S OFFICE. DAWN.
They walk into a large office overlooking a courtyard. The early morning sun is just lighting the office, its grand dimensions, its confident tasteful decor.

CHARLES: So I can do coffee . . . I like to think it's the only drinkable coffee in the Foreign Office – and I've got some grapefruit. (*He holds up two grapefruit, grinning.*) And of course, inevitably, some white wine – which *I'm* going to have.

REBECCA*'s eyes flash at this, as* CHARLES *takes a bottle from the fridge.*

DANIEL: Great office! (*He sinks into a comfortable chair.*)

REBECCA: Charles is head of all things European – very, very cutting edge at the moment.

CHARLES: Not quite *all* things . . . (*to* DANIEL.) I've been abroad a lot up till now, I was due to do my two years desk-bound. So here I am . . .

He sits at his desk with his legs up, as he peels grapefruit with knife.

DANIEL: This is just what I imagined . . . ! You know – I've been trying to guess what you two did . . . and of course it had to be Public Service . . . speaking loads of languages probably . . . Grand desk, powerful jobs . . . a big room with pillars!

CHARLES: And grapefruit . . .

DANIEL: It's so right for you, Charles . . . !

CHARLES (*smiles*): And he's only known me a few hours.

REBECCA *has opened the doors at the other end of the office that lead into a conference room.*

REBECCA: I'm much too old to stay up all night!

She takes off her shoes and stretches out on a table in the conference room.

REBECCA: Jesus . . . that's better . . .

DANIEL *watches* REBECCA *from his chair, as she is stretched out on the table.* CHARLES*'s voice is running on in the background, getting fainter.*

CHARLES: Isn't it amazing . . . we're completely alone here except for security . . . I know it's a *little* early on a

Sunday but there's no round-the-clock working here . . .
We close in on DANIEL*'s face.* CHARLES*'s voice cuts out.*

We see the photo of the little prince on the stairs. And then we're suddenly moving in live action with the little prince down a grand passage. Subjective shot, moving with the little boy. He enters one of the large reception rooms of the London mansion. REBECCA, *as she is now, is sitting on a window seat. The room is full of sunlight.* REBECCA *is smiling.*

REBECCA: You *really* want this house, don't you . . .? You want it to be YOURS!

Suddenly the adult DANIEL *is kissing her passionately. Their bodies close. Then entwined. A powerful extreme attraction. Their faces and bodies together really intense. As* DANIEL *kisses her, we hear the noise that he first heard in the passage of the hotel, from the room next door, the sound of anguish and rage.*

DANIEL (*as he is kissing* REBECCA, *the noise echoing*): Of course – I knew it was *you* . . .

DANIEL wakes with a start, the noise is still with him for a moment. He sees that REBECCA *is staring at him from the table in the other room, watching him wake.*

REBECCA: Bad dream . . . ?

DANIEL: No, quite the contrary . . .

CHARLES: The coffee's nearly ready . . . (*He's sipping the white wine.*) Do I have any takers for the grapefruit?

DANIEL picks up two quarters of grapefruit and moves towards REBECCA *in the other room. She takes one of them as she lies on the table.*

REBECCA: We better say goodbye.

DANIEL (*taken aback*): Goodbye? . . .

REBECCA: Yes, I've got to leave today – there's a bit of trouble at work . . .

DANIEL: It's Sunday.

REBECCA: Don't worry, now we've met, I'm sure we'll keep

70

in touch.

DANIEL: You can't go.

REBECCA: I can't go . . . ?

DANIEL: Not before the banquet. It's forbidden.

REBECCA: I've got special permission.

DANIEL (*he thinks quickly*): Besides – Stephen's got something for you.

REBECCA (*her eyes flick*): What sort of thing?

DANIEL: A surprise . . . something as good as my picture . . .

REBECCA: I haven't seen your picture . . . anyway, I can't deal with Stephen today, being lectured by him –

DANIEL: Don't worry, I'll get it for you – you just have to promise to stay for it . . .

INT. HOTEL PASSAGE. DAY.

DANIEL *moves along the hotel passage; we can hear* STEPHEN*'s voice booming out from the end of the passage leading* DANIEL *on.*

STEPHEN'S VOICE: Many people think of pedigree hunters as sort of detectives – except *we* start with the present and continue to go backwards – and yes there is sometimes a thrill attached . . .

DANIEL *reaches the half-open door, and stands in the doorway watching. He can see a motley collection of relations listening to* STEPHEN *including* VIOLET *and* EDITH, *the two genial sisters. And right in the front row is his mother,* ESTHER, *who is watching* STEPHEN *very closely, obviously deeply involved. She is even taking notes.* DANIEL *watches his mother, fascinated.*

STEPHEN: And just like a detective too, we can be seduced by false trails . . . we are now very familiar with how wonderful the Internet has proved in helping us in our research with our family trees – but the *same* mistakes

71

occur there too . . .

His arms jerk up in emphasis. DANIEL *smiles. He looks down and realises he's playing with the child's shoe, the one he took from the big house.*

STEPHEN: Just because it's the same surname and the right region of the country, and the village seems right –
DOESN'T MEAN YOU'RE RELATED TO THEM.
People have crossed the world to find lost relations and have been bitterly disappointed.

ESTHER (*raising her hand*): But it's worth following clues – however vague they are, isn't it . . . ? If you can remember your parents saying – for instance – I'm making this example up . . . 'I always thought there was something going on between my father and the family at the manor . . .' It's worth having a look, isn't it?

STEPHEN: Absolutely – take every turning!

Of course, illegitimacy is our great hurdle. (*His arms jerk.*) Our stiffest test . . . because it was so common and nearly always there's no trace in the records . . .

We cut to the audience coming out. DANIEL *watches his mother emerge – she is carrying a big pile of books.*

DANIEL: You looked really into it, Mum!

ESTHER: So you've been lurking here watching me, have you?

DANIEL (*indicating the books*): You're turning into a student . . .

ESTHER: Stephen let me have these. (*She notices* DANIEL *wearing the long leather coat. She touches it.*) What's this . . . ?

At this moment Stephen passes them at a rapid pace.

STEPHEN: Excuse me . . .! (*He shoots off down the passage.*)

DANIEL: Got to dash –

He leaves his mother and runs after Stephen down the passage catching him up with difficulty.

DANIEL: Stephen – I need to ask you something . . .

STEPHEN: I'm in a bit of a rush now – I need to have a wash –
So . . . if you don't mind, seeing that . . .

INT. STEPHEN'S ROOM. AFTERNOON.

DANIEL *is gazing around* STEPHEN*'s room which is full of stacks
of files, computers, old books and ledgers, boxes stuffed with
information, like a whole portable archive.*

STEPHEN *is having a shower, the door open to the bathroom,
as he washes with great thoroughness. We cut between* DANIEL
staring at the archive in the room and STEPHEN *in the shower.*

DANIEL (*raising his voice above the noise of the water*): I love
the picture you found of me.
STEPHEN (*soaping under his arms*): Good . . . the only one we
have of you, but it is a corker, yes . . .

DANIEL *moves over to the files and the computer. He opens a
folder.*

STEPHEN (*from the shower*): What are you looking at? . . .
careful in there . . . I would rather you didn't touch
anything.

DANIEL *is startled because* STEPHEN *can only hear him, not
see him from the shower.*

DANIEL: I was just amazed at all this stuff you've brought
with you . . .
STEPHEN: I like to have things at my fingertips.

DANIEL *is rifling through the files, stops just in time as* STEPHEN
comes into the room. STEPHEN *is dripping wet and naked
except for a towel.*

STEPHEN: That's better . . .!

*He sits on the end of the bed, and then begins to examine his
very clean feet.*

STEPHEN: So what did you need to see me so urgently about?
DANIEL: I wondered . . . or rather Rebecca wondered, she's

73

in a mini crisis about work at the moment, but she really wanted to know if you had anything for her as good as my picture – something startling, she doesn't know about?

STEPHEN (*looking at him disapprovingly*): 'Something startling' . . . ?

DANIEL: Yes.

STEPHEN: I only respond to direct questions, from the person concerned. Obviously. To protect confidentiality.

DANIEL: This is a direct request – it's just via me . . .

STEPHEN *watches him for a moment.*

STEPHEN: You want to know what the most surprising thing in the room is? . . . The most startling?

DANIEL: Yes. (*Staring around.*) Of course I do.

STEPHEN: Then – it's about me.

DANIEL (*unable to conceal his disappointment*): About you . . . ?

STEPHEN: Without a doubt . . . I can see that's not what you wanted to hear.

DANIEL: No. No . . . that's great . . .

DANIEL *looks at the semi-naked comic figure of* STEPHEN, *then gazes round the room.*

DANIEL: I'm trying hard to think what you're referring to . . .

STEPHEN (*drying himself*): Over there . . . that book . . . no, the red one . . . open it.

DANIEL *hesitates by the old books that have been beautifully cleaned.*

DANIEL: I'm afraid to touch anything . . . they're so clean.

STEPHEN: You can touch that . . .

DANIEL *opens the book. Something flutters out.*

STEPHEN: Careful!

DANIEL *picks up the fluttering piece of paper. It is tracing paper with a very faint family tree on it written in brown ink. He can see the names are German.*

DANIEL: This is it? . . . What's so surprising?

STEPHEN: Because it's all lies.

DANIEL (*just glancing at it*): All lies . . .?

STEPHEN: Look at it . . . What does it tell you?

DANIEL: It looks like maybe the work of a child –

STEPHEN: When in the last hundred years would you really want to make up a whole family tree?

DANIEL (*staring at intently*): Of course – in Nazi Germany . . .

STEPHEN (*pointing*): Orange file . . . no . . .*Orange* file . . .

DANIEL *opens the orange file. It has only one page in it, written in ink in German. And there's a faded photo of a boy about twelve.* DANIEL *looks at the boy and at the family tree. The tracing paper rustles in the draught. As it does we see a grainy flashback, a classroom of boys. One of the class is reciting his family names and his family birthplace . . . 'Wolfgang Haubrichs . . . Spandau . . .'*

STEPHEN (*VO*): If you are a Jewish family in Nazi Germany just before the outbreak of war . . . and you don't look particularly Jewish – then a false identity is a possibility . . . a whole new genealogy . . . it's extremely risky, of course –

We settle on one BOY *near the back of the class. We cut back to the present. It is the same* BOY *in the picture.* DANIEL *looks across at* STEPHEN.

STEPHEN (*during his line we cut back to the flashback*): And he had to know it off by heart . . . but not so well it seemed too glib . . .

BOY: Dieter Rohl . . . Passau . . .

STEPHEN (*VO*): So your father's name and birthplace was easy . . . and your mother's maiden name was easy . . .

BOY: Christa Vetter . . . Neuruppin . . .

We stay on the BOY's *face, staring, intense, but trying not to give anything away.*

STEPHEN (*VO*): But how confident should you be about her mother's maiden name and birthplace . . .?

BOY (*hesitantly*): Kirstin Huber . . . Meisenheim . . .

The only sounds in the flashback are the children's voices reciting names and towns.

We see the TEACHER *beckoning the* BOY. *The* BOY *comes to the front of the class . . . the* TEACHER *holds the* BOY's *head, twists it one way and then the other, opens the* BOY's *mouth like inspecting a horse. Takes a tape measure and measures the* BOY's *skull.*

Then he looks up and addresses the class, beaming triumphantly. We hear his voice in faint German.

STEPHEN (*VO*): And he says – 'This is a wonderful example of an Aryan head!'

We cut back to DANIEL. *He is staring at the names in the brown ink.*

DANIEL (*softly*): Using a family tree as a weapon . . . to fight with . . .

We cut to the passages of the school. We hear the litany of family names and places on the soundtrack. At first, the BOY's *voice, and then a young girl's voice joins in . . . the litany like a musical soundtrack. We follow the* BOY *down the school passage. A dark tall figure comes up behind him.*

STEPHEN (*VO*): A priest teaches at the school, religious instruction . . . He comes upon the boy one day reading a book. A book about giraffes. The priest befriends the boy –

We cut to a library with books. The PRIEST *is working at a ledger writing names, and the* BOY *is lifting a very large book for the* PRIEST *and glancing at other books eagerly.*

STEPHEN: The priest needed somebody to help him move books, but he also liked the company, as he spends most of the time making a new registers, all the parishioners' antecedents – the authorities were determined to know the correct descent of every single citizen in public service.

We hear the litany of children's voices reciting names and places.

STEPHEN: And the boy wanted to keep the priest company because he loved books, especially the beautiful old animal books . . .

We see the inside of a book, magnificent nineteenth-century plates of reptiles, huge snakes wrapped round trees, crocodiles, lizards.

> *Then we cut to* DANIEL *in the present, with the same book, turning the pages.*

DANIEL: He didn't tell the priest!? He can't have told the priest the truth, can he . . . ?!

The litany of place names, the children's voices lead us back.

> *The* BOY *sits at one end of the great table, facing the* PRIEST, *with a huge ledger open between them.*

STEPHEN (*VO*): One day he told the priest . . . because he wanted to tell someone . . . it was too big a secret . . . (*We see the* BOY *smiling at the* PRIEST. *The* PRIEST *smiles back.*) Three days later . . .

> *The* BOY *and his sister, a* LITTLE GIRL, *are walking along a passage of a nineteenth-century apartment block.*

STEPHEN (*VO*): Whether it is a complete coincidence or not, the boy is coming back from school with his young sister –

We see POLICE *at the door of his apartment talking to his* MOTHER.

STEPHEN: He instinctively tells the little girl to run away.

The BOY *heads towards the door of the apartment. We cut back to* DANIEL *staring at the* BOY*'s face.*

DANIEL: Why didn't they both run . . . ?

STEPHEN: Would you have run . . . ? Left your parents? It's much easier to tell somebody else to . . .

77

The camera peers down the old nineteenth-century staircase with its iron ornamental balustrade. Footsteps clattering down, the vanishing figure of the LITTLE GIRL *getting smaller and smaller.*

STEPHEN (*VO*): The little girl disappears . . . and although the police search . . . and secretly the family search . . . she had gone. Vanished off the face of the earth.

The camera tracks down the well of the stairs into the blackness and then dissolves into the passages of the apartment block.

STEPHEN (*VO*): In fact, she hadn't gone far . . .

We cut back to STEPHEN *sitting bolt upright.* DANIEL *watches him intensely.*

STEPHEN: She had an amazing piece of luck, she had run into a flat at the bottom of the stairs, and the elderly lady there had hidden her . . . and then a few hours later the lady took her across town to her sister, her childless sister, who had always longed for children . . . this woman fell in love with the girl . . . passed her off as her niece . . . but in fact became the little girl's mother . . . (*We see the* LITTLE GIRL *sitting with the middle-aged lady, in some tearooms during the war, eating a small piece of cake. We close in on* STEPHEN.) Unbelievable good fortune. But what the girl still had to do . . .

We cut to another apartment staircase less grand, with peeling walls. Out of the shadows comes the LITTLE GIRL, *reciting as she comes a litany of family names and place names, committing them to memory.*

STEPHEN: She had to teach herself a whole new family tree . . .

LITTLE GIRL: Susanne Flatauer. *Darmstadt* . . . Petra Schlupp . . . *Kesseldorf* . . . Tobias Ruchardt . . . *Koblenz.*

DANIEL *mouths the name of 'Tobias Ruchardt' as the camera moves across the brown ink of the fake family tree, in its childish writing.*

DANIEL: So this is the *girl's* tree . . . ! (*He looks at Stephen.*)
She was your mother, wasn't she?

STEPHEN: Yes, indeed . . . she was my mother . . .

DANIEL (*quiet for a moment, moved*): But did the boy survive?
Did he – because the book is here! He did, didn't he!?

STEPHEN: Oh no, the rest of the family died. The book is
here, because after the war –

A YOUNG WOMAN *in her twenties moves through a church
hall where a jumble sale is taking place. The same* PRIEST
presides over the sale. A lot of old books are spread out. The
YOUNG WOMAN *watches the* PRIEST *for a moment from a
distance. Then she goes up to him. The* PRIEST *tries to
interest in her a book on women's fashion. But the* YOUNG
WOMAN *picks up the big red book on reptiles. The* YOUNG
WOMAN *insists that this is the book she wants. The* PRIEST
looks puzzled. Their eyes meet. The YOUNG WOMAN *moves
off, and we see the* PRIEST *watching her disappear into the
crowd.*

We cut back to the present. DANIEL *instinctively puts the
book down. It's as if at that moment it is zinging with the
past. It disturbs him. He looks across at* STEPHEN.
STEPHEN *has tears in his eyes.*

STEPHEN: But I never really talked to my mother about the
story, until she was dying. It's quite amazing how one
leaves these things too late . . .

That's why I have become a pedigree hunter, the
archive man of the family . . . I have the zeal of a
convert.

DANIEL: Yes . . . I can understand that.

*He pauses for a moment very thoughtful, staring at all the
things from the past.*

DANIEL: Maybe that's happening to me too . . .

STEPHEN: Anyway, that's the story – that's the best I can do

79

for you, Daniel.

DANIEL: Thank you . . .

He stares at the red book. He hesitates and then can't help mentioning it.

DANIEL: And Rebecca?

STEPHEN *looks up, his tone very final.*

STEPHEN: Not today . . .! Not before the banquet!

INT. BALLROOM. EVENING.

High shot of the ballroom, a series of circular tables, heavily decorated. A few waiters are doing final arrangements. Otherwise the ballroom is empty except for ALICE *who is standing at one end surveying the scene.*

INT. RAYMOND AND ESTHER'S ROOM. EVENING.

A close-up of RAYMOND's *eyes springing open. The room is dark, he is sweating. He feels strangely disorientated. He looks around in the dark.* ESTHER *is in the bathroom, just the glow of light through the half-open door. From* RAYMOND's *POV both* ESTHER *and the room look distorted for a second. The darkness closing in.* RAYMOND *makes himself sit up.*

RAYMOND: I had no idea where I was then – or what was happening . . . What time is it?

ESTHER: Time you were ready.

RAYMOND: Now?! . . . I thought it was about lunchtime! . . . (*He glances round the dark room.*) That means I missed my appointment with Peter . . . (*We stay close on* RAYMOND's *face.*) I was having an extraordinary dream about my parents . . . (*quiet*) everyone was shouting . . . I'm surprised I've got any voice left . . . !

INT. BALLROOM. EVENING.

The ballroom is lying in readiness. It is empty except for the waiters and now REBECCA, *who is moving among the tables, she is glancing at the place names. When we get closer we can hear her muttering.*

REBECCA: Jesus, these people are boringly arranged . . . (*She is picking up place names and swapping them round.*)

INT. EDITH'S AND VIOLET'S ROOM/PASSAGE. EVENING.
EDITH *and* VIOLET *are dressed up in voluminous dresses, fussing round the room.*

VIOLET: How is she? . . . Is she all right?
EDITH: She's going to be fine.
They are both looking through the half-open door to the passage where GRACE *is sitting bolt upright on a small sofa. She is in a dark evening dress. Her stern unyielding expression.*
Further along the passage IRVING *is opening the door of his room to the fleshy* SIDNEY. *Both are in dinner jackets,* IRVING *just tying his red bow tie.*
IRVING: Come on, Sid, have a tipple . . . something to help you through the banquet . . .
SIDNEY: Excellent. I thought one might be on offer here.
IRVING (*indicating* GRACE *in the passage*): Amazing who you are pleased to discover you're related to – and who you're not . . .!
SIDNEY (*gazing at* GRACE): And who you've forgotten all about . . .

INT. DANIEL'S ROOM. EVENING.
DANIEL *is standing in is dinner jacket looking at himself in the
mirror. We see the little prince standing on the stairs gazing,
confident and haughty.* DANIEL *adopts the same posture in front
of the mirror. He looks great in his dinner jacket.*

DANIEL: Careful – Don't turn into a pushy little shit . . .
The eyes of the little prince very big, staring straight at him.
DANIEL *grins.*
DANIEL: One the other hand, one never knows . . . !

INT. ANTE-ROOM OF BALLROOM. EVENING.
*The ante-room of the ballroom is a sea of dinner jackets and
evening dresses. The* SIBLINGS' MOTHER *is staring at the table
plan. A few place numbers next to the names have been altered in
pen.*

SIBLINGS' MOTHER: Poppy can't even get the place numbers
right! Somebody's had to alter them . . . !
DANIEL *enters. He sees* REBECCA *looking radiant standing
among a group of family members in dinner jackets. He goes
up to her.*
DANIEL: I've failed . . . Stephen wouldn't give me anything –
for you. Not tonight . . .
REBECCA: So you've kept me here under false pretences . . .
(*She is staring around.*) Actually Charles said I *had* to be
here.
DANIEL (*producing the shoe out of his pocket*): My lucky charm
. . . maybe somebody here will remember it.
REBECCA: It's like Cinderella in reverse – you know who it fits
– You just don't know who gave it to you . . .
DANIEL*'s attention is suddenly caught by the sight of his
father. The appalling spectacle of his father being the only*

82

man there not in a dinner jacket. RAYMOND *is wearing a
battered old jacket.* DANIEL *moves across.*

ESTHER: Don't look at me – there is absolutely nothing I
could do about it . . .

RAYMOND: I don't know what the fuss is about –

DANIEL: You've gotta change.

RAYMOND: You can't be serious – this is just the family . . .
And I never wear a dinner jacket . . . !

DANIEL (*with real force*): *You are going to change.*

INT. RAYMOND'S ROOM. EVENING.
RAYMOND *is pulling on his dinner jacket with some difficulty, as
if he is already drunk.* DANIEL *is helping him.*

RAYMOND: Can you? . . .

DANIEL: I can't *believe* you've done this – what were you
trying to prove?

RAYMOND: Can you pass the . . . (*Fumbling for the word.*)
The squashed thing . . . the dead thing . . . (*Pointing at
crumpled bow tie.*)

DANIEL: What – the tie? . . . (*Loud.*) You mean THE TIE?!
You can't even say that . . .? (*Beginning to fasten the bow
tie for his father.*) How've you managed to drink so much
already?

INT. BALLROOM. EVENING.
The banquet is in full flow. DANIEL *is sitting on the top table,*
ERNEST'*s table, with* REBECCA. ERNEST *is flanked by his
Lebanese wife* NAZIK *and his daughter* MARTINA. *Both women
are wearing diamonds.* ERNEST *is looking across at* DANIEL,
trying to work out what he is doing on his table. DANIEL *is
looking back, smiling, delighted to be there.*

ERNEST: Very pleased to find you on this table . . . I just don't think we know each other . . . ?

DANIEL: I'm Daniel. Raymond's son . . . We live just outside London . . .

The moon-faced son PETER *is also at the table beaming.*
DANIEL *smiles back, feeling part of an inner circle.*

We cut to POPPY *surveying the banquet, looking horrified. She turns to her* BOY ASSISTANT.

POPPY: Something strange has happened . . . People are sitting at the wrong tables! . . . I spent so much time on the right grouping. HOW CAN THIS HAVE HAPPENED?

ALICE *and* RAYMOND *sit opposite each other on another table.* ESTHER *next to* RAYMOND. ALICE *looking equally puzzled at who has ended up sitting at her table.* RAYMOND *notices this.*

RAYMOND: So I was wrong – we're sharing another meal almost immediately.

ALICE: Yes . . . I'm very pleased, naturally.

RAYMOND (*to* ESTHER): I don't think in a million years she expected us to be on her table . . .

ALICE: I don't know why you should feel that, Raymond. But as it happens it *is* a surprise . . . a good one, of course.

POPPY *is getting more and more agitated, seen from* DANIEL*'s POV.*

DANIEL (*to* REBECCA): It looks like Poppy thinks somebody has played around with her table plan . . .

REBECCA *stares straight at him. Their eyes meet.*

REBECCA: What a childish thing to do . . . Why should anybody bother to do that?

DANIEL: Who knows? . . . Fortunate for me though.

We cut to CHARLES *appearing on a dais at one end of the ballroom, tapping the microphone and hushing the banqueting.* CHARLES *sparkles as a natural master of ceremonies.*

CHARLES: So I'm here, I'm here because as we all know,
Ernest our host (*grateful applause*) doesn't like making
speeches (*he grins*) although we'll see about that . . .

But I hope a lot of you will take this chance of doing
so yourselves . . . the idea here is a sort of family karaoke
– what's been happening to you . . . Come up here and
tell us please – this is your bulletin board . . . don't be
shy . . . ! In a family so rich in history and events we
should have a whale of a time . . . !

So – who's going to be really brave? . . . who's going
to be first?

We see from CHARLES*'s POV all the different faces, the
fleshy* IRVING *and* SIDNEY *presiding over a table,* VIOLET,
EDITH *and* GRACE *on another.* STEPHEN *sitting bolt
upright with a notepad next to him, the missing man quietly
staring ahead.* DANIEL *is staring around too, recognising
some memorable faces from the old photos in the mansion.*

MARTINA *suddenly leaps up from the table and bounds to
the microphone. She launches off with total confidence.*

MARTINA: Hello . . . hello, everyone! I'll be first! I want to tell
you all – my life is so full and so exciting at the moment,
with the swimming, and the little touch of modelling I've
been doing, and the dancing and the riding, my new
horse is called Jupiter, and of course the *studying*! Where
on earth to begin? Maybe I'll begin by talking about my
wonderful fiance and how we first met. Where do you
think it happened? Can you guess?! . . . Somebody have
a guess?! (*She stares down and beams at them all.*) . . . It
was actually and very appropriately at my absolutely
favourite restaurant! . . .

ALICE: Such a modest girl!

RAYMOND: Alice, you should be up there . . . (*to the table
smiling.*) She has a wild side I've discovered, one the rest
of the world should know about!

We cut to IRVING *who is now at the microphone.*

IRVING: So . . . (*He stares at the audience.*) Seeing me up here
I know a lot of you'll be thinking – at last we may find
out what he really does with his time, what he's actually
up to? Well, I would hate to dispel the faint air of
mystery that I seem to give off – if that's the right
expression . . . (*he smiles*) So I'm not going to – except to
say things continue to go well. But I *am* going to offer
the family two little slices of advice of a financial nature .
. . (*he grins.*)
Absolutely free of charge . . . The first is – keep an eye
on Malaya . . . this is my hot up to the minute tip –
straight from the horse's mouth . . . And the second is –
never, ever underestimate people's desire to buy
property near water . . . take advantage of worldwide
flooding . . . nobody ever went broke thinking about
houses and water. So what today might seem like a
stagnant pond or a right sewer of a canal – tomorrow
could be liquid gold. My second red hot tip therefore is –
sniff out that water! . . .

We cut to RAYMOND *who is sweating, his manner febrile.*
He stares around the ballroom, at all the faces of the family.
We cut to MR DEGAZI *who is now at the microphone.*

MR DEGAZI: So I just want to thank you from the bottom of
my heart – all you wonderful people who have asked to
see me! I can't possibly see you all but I feel profoundly
pleased and touched – and I'm working my way through
the list . . . bear with me . . .

RAYMOND *is staring at* CHARLES *and then at* REBECCA.

RAYMOND (*to* ALICE): Amazing the brother and sister . . .
golden children, aren't they?! . . . He is so charming and
all the rest of it, and she is *fantastic* . . . ! What's more the
mother looks quite the dullest person here . . . !
(*Watching* DANIEL *and* REBECCA.) And it looks like my

son is right in there . . . Quick work, mate!

ALICE *is staring towards* REBECCA *and* DANIEL. *We see she's deeply interested.*

ALICE: Yes, I'd noticed that too . . .

CHARLES (*from microphone*): We're doing well here . . . So who is next . . .?

From DANIEL's *POV* RAYMOND *is stirring.*

DANIEL: No . . . please . . . (*He sees his mother has turned away from* RAYMOND, *talking to her neighbour, seemingly paying no attention.*) Why isn't she stopping him? . . . (*Under his breath.*) Don't let this happen . . .

VIOLET *stands up,* DANIEL *looks immediately relieved, and then suddenly* RAYMOND *is on his feet, and lurching towards the dais, passing Violet.* DANIEL *looks on appalled.*

REBECCA (*softly*): You're not going to rugby tackle him . . . are you?

RAYMOND *reaches the microphone.*

RAYMOND: So I'm Raymond . . . not seen you lot for a while! Some of you will remember my father Lionel pretty vividly – (*He grins.*) Yeah, I see you do! . . .

We cut between DANIEL *watching his father, imploring him with his eyes to stop, and* RAYMOND.

RAYMOND: My papa made the dramatic decision to settle in Hillingdon. I know a lot of you will not be able to readily place Hillingdon . . . the Underground map . . . Picture the Underground map . . .

He squiggles an imaginary map in the air.

RAYMOND: And then go up, no further . . . Up, up and away . . . as far as you can imagine, up to the thinnest branches – to Pinner and Beyond! Now even further . . . to Ruislip Manor and the magical Hillingdon . . .

He pinpoints it in the air. Nervous laughter from the tables.

RAYMOND: Not a bad place actually!

DANIEL *suddenly gets up. The sound from the ballroom*

begins to cut out as DANIEL *crosses between the tables and heads for the door. Then we see his face turning in the shadows outside the ballroom. We see a high shot of the banquet, and then faces staring nervously up towards* RAYMOND. *We move in very closely on* DANIEL *as he realises disaster may be beckoning, but he is powerless to stop it.*

We see the WAITERS *receive the signal to move forward with the coffee. At the moment they spread through the ballroom the live sound comes back with an abrupt cut.*

RAYMOND: I want just to return to that question 'IS EVERYTHING OK . . .?' (*He grins.*) Because we're all family here after all . . . even though it's been so many years. And Charles has said we're involved in a sort of family karaoke here, and as we've heard some nice easy listening so far, maybe it's time for some HARD ROCK.

Shots of ESTHER *and* ALICE *watching,* RAYMOND *moving on stage.*

RAYMOND: Of course, some of you already know about the bold experiment that went wrong – and there's no shame in that, I hear you say . . . and indeed in one way that is true . . .

So why do I mention it now . . . ?

I became obsessed with *age* – and looking round this room I thought that might be of some interest . . . people having to end their working lives earlier and earlier . . . fifty-one, fifty-two – on the scrap heap. That's not a place that most of you are familiar with, I realise! . . . whatever your age . . . (*sharp smile*) but it exists . . . Oh yes . . . !

Tears begin to form in DANIEL's *eyes as he witnesses the spectacle his father is making.*

RAYMOND: People get told – 'You're too old! You're much too old, you're incredibly too old!' . . . But I hired them!

And it was great! And then when I tried to borrow money *I* was told – BUT *YOU'RE* FAR TOO OLD . . . You foolish shit . . . crawl away, old man.' (*He smiles.*) Or words to that effect . . . (*He half sings the word into the microphone.*) Foolish . . . (*Singing.*) I was kind of foolish . . .

He moves with the microphone despite his state – he is a charismatic dangerous performer.

RAYMOND: Charles has said there's a lot of history here – too bloody right there is – and that uncorked something . . .

I want to take you back . . . No, no this won't take long . . .

My father sent me to rather a sad old boarding school when I was eight . . . lovely old house in the country though. It had an orchard . . . and the orchard was full of hedgehogs . . . Oh yes, you know like a story-book England, hedgehogs with apples sticking on their backs . . . like in – what's she called – Beatrix . . . Beatrix . . . Beatrix Blyton . . . No, that's wrong . . . Come on – (*He fumbles for the word, somebody calls out Beatrix Potter, he doesn't seem to hear. . . .*) Yes. Beatrix . . . you know who I mean . . . (*He lurches on stage, then recovers.*)

Shots of members of the family watching him. And DANIEL *seeing their faces.*

RAYMOND: The headmaster of the school was a real prick . . So for a dare I got a hedgehog, went into the school with it under my jumper . . . along the corridors, into his private study – nobody there, it was wonderfully easy . . . The idea was to stick it in the drawer of his desk – the boring old fart . . .! And just as I was doing that, horror of horrors, the door flies open – and this is totally and absolutely true – and there were MY PARENTS with the headmaster, and I'm standing there, in the most forbidden place in the school, with a hedgehog just

89

pulled out of my jumper, and the bloody animal's peeing and shitting all over his private papers . . . And there's nothing, absolutely *nothing* I can do . . . I'm helpless. I'm transfixed. And my parents, who up to that moment thought of me as a model pupil, are of course stunned . . . *We see the picture of his father.*

RAYMOND: My father . . .

> RAYMOND *stops. Silence. People are staring at him in embarrassed fascination. Almost holding their breath.*
> And I felt so . . . so utterly foolish . . . (*he half sings*) kind of foolish . . .
>
> (*Quiet.*) Never did discover what they were doing there . . . My parents . . .
>
> RAYMOND *stares at the microphone. He makes a strange noise.*

RAYMOND: Can we do depression? Karaoke depression and despair? . . . Don't know how you'd do that . . . but there ought to be a way . . . not just upbeat happy pappy things . . . but saying I too have been there . . . in hell . . .

> *He stares wildly at them for a moment. Then he sits on the dais, his voice becoming more and more slurred.* DANIEL*'s face staring, shocked, pale. The ballroom is deadly quiet.*

RAYMOND: Do I have anything up my jumper tonight? . . . And since you ask . . . (*He takes off his jacket, slips his hand inside his shirt, slurred smile.*) Up my shirt . . . is the secret of everything . . . Just can't remember what you call it . . .

> *He blows into the microphone. Then he speaks out but his voice makes only hoarse incomprehensible sounds, as he rocks backwards and forwards with the microphone.*

RAYMOND: Excuse me . . . got to pay a call . . .

> RAYMOND *lurches off the dais, almost falling over and disappears out of the ballroom, into the kitchens, through the crowd of* WAITERS.

INT. KITCHENS. EVENING.

We cut to the commotion in the kitchens. DANIEL *is moving through the throng of people, trying to reach his father. The young* WAITER, *from the beginning, looks very startled and upset.* RAYMOND *is lying on the floor of the kitchen on his side,* ESTHER *is kneeling by him. She looks very shocked.*

ESTHER: They're getting a doctor . . . I think he may have had a slight stroke . . .

> RAYMOND *beckons* DANIEL *close. When* DANIEL*'s face is right up to his,* RAYMOND *points at all the desserts surrounding him in fluted glasses, decorated by Cape gooseberries.* RAYMOND *indicates the Cape gooseberries.*

RAYMOND (*whispering*): Never known what the hell those things are called . . .?!

> *A* DOCTOR *appears, pushing people out of the way, very brisk.*

DOCTOR: Excuse me . . . could I have everyone – and that means *everyone* – out of here right now . . .! (*To* DANIEL.) You too!

> DANIEL *is being pushed back by the throng.*

DANIEL: But I'm his son . . .

> DANIEL *is watching the various faces of the family in front of him. Startled looks, people trying to work out what has happened. He sees* ALICE *helping to get the kitchens cleared . . . Way in the distance* DANIEL *glimpses* REBECCA *standing at the end of one of the passages.*
>
> *Suddenly the fleshy-faced* SIDNEY *is right beside him.* DANIEL *can't help flinching.* SIDNEY *is the last person he wants to see.* SIDNEY*'s tone is concerned but knowing.*

SIDNEY: He'll be OK, won't he? He *has* to be OK . . . I thought it was a good speech . . . I might be the only one . . . but I did.

> *The swirl of the family behind him.* SIDNEY*'s face close. A*

very knowing look.

SIDNEY: Of course, if you have to stay around for a bit –
That's no great hardship, is it?!

His face even closer. His piercing eyes.

SIDNEY: Just remember one thing, Daniel . . . everybody
always lies . . .

Credits.

PERFECT STRANGERS

Part Two

OPENING SEQUENCE.

The photos of DANIEL's GRANDFATHER *dancing on the lawn. A sequence of several photos and details from within the photos, the stone beasts, the garden, the expression of joy on the* GRANDFATHER's *face.*

Then we dissolve into the picture of the Little Prince staring straight out at us.

INT. HOSPITAL. NIGHT.

We cut from the purposeful stare of the little boy to DANIEL, *dressed in his dinner jacket, walking urgently through the accident and emergency department of the hospital, passing the hospital flotsam of a Sunday night. People bleeding and people drunk, people in pain, young men rocking backwards and forwards on benches.*

We come upon ALICE *and* ESTHER *in their evening dress, and in a corner* PETER *is sitting, also still in his dinner jacket, with a peaceful look on his face.*

ESTHER (*immediately on seeing* DANIEL): It's OK . . . I think
  it's OK. They're giving him a full examination now . . .
DANIEL: Good – great . . . they're doing it now? How long till
  they tell us . . . ?
ALICE: It won't be long.
DANIEL: Do they know what happened?
ESTHER: They think it's a mild stoke.
DANIEL (*very speedy*): Right . . . (*suddenly, seeing* PETER.)
  How come everybody got here before me?
ALICE: Ernest's driver brought us – we looked for you . . .
DANIEL: I got cornered by some talkative relations, at the
  worst possible moment –
  *A blood-splattered drunk appears at the other end of the
  corridor, and seeing them standing there in their evening*

95

dress, starts haranguing them. 'So this is where I should be!
This is where to get service!' etc.

As the night casualties move restlessly in the depth of field,
ESTHER *is summoned by a doctor.*

ALICE (*seeing how agitated* DANIEL *is, softly*): Don't worry,
your father is going to be all right. (*She moves.*) There is
rather a temperamental coffee machine here, I've already
had a fight with it. Do you want a cup?

DANIEL (*moving over to coffee machine*): Right, yes – (*He
reaches into his pocket for coins.*)

ALICE: Don't be silly . . . (*She puts some coins in.*) I found the
secret is – it takes much longer than you expect . . .
DANIEL *with* ALICE, *staring at the coffee machine, waiting
for it to work.*

DANIEL: I'm so sorry . . .

ALICE: What are you sorry about?

DANIEL: That the banquet was interrupted . . . unavoidably
of course . . . But I'm so sorry your big occasion –

ALICE: And thank God it was interrupted! That family
karaoke, has anybody ever had a worse idea?

DANIEL(*smiling with relief*): Probably not . . . (*Indicating the
coffee machine.*) I see what you mean . . .

ALICE: Just when you've given up hope . . .
The coffee begins to appear. ALICE *eyes the drunks at the end
of the passage.*

ALICE (*softly*): Daniel, your father will obviously need a little
time to recover and the best possible care –

DANIEL: Yes, my mum and I, one of us may have to stop
working for a bit –

ALICE: The family would really like to help with all this.
There is a flat, very near here, that Ernest isn't currently
using, because he's living in the country. There is a staff
there who could cook for him and everything. And we
have an excellent family doctor –

PETER *is smiling from his corner.*

DANIEL: Sounds perfect, but –

ALICE: Your father might feel . . . your father is –

DANIEL: A proud obstinate bastard?! (*He smiles.*) Yes.

ALICE: We want him to have the very best – now he's here
among us. (*She looks at* DANIEL.) We don't want to leave
things unfinished . . .

ESTHER *appears, beckoning him.*

ESTHER: Daniel?

We cut to RAYMOND *lying asleep in a hospital bed.*

ESTHER (*softly, whispering*): He just needs rest . . . somebody
watching over him . . . (*she turns to* DANIEL.) We'll take
it in turns. I'll do the first watch . . .

INT. HOTEL PASSAGES. NIGHT.

*A vivid rather hallucinatory feel as all the characters wander the
passages, coming out of each other's rooms, a sense of their
evening dislocated. They are all still in their evening dress.*

DANIEL *is approaching, down the red passage, with* ALICE. *As
soon as people see* DANIEL *they pepper him with questions.*

POPPY: How are things? What's the latest? Is there anything I
can do? Does anybody need transport?

DANIEL: It's OK . . . he'll be OK.

VIOLET'*s rosy-cheeked face pops up.*

VIOLET: That's such good news!

IRVING: Everybody's been rampaging around looking for
news . . . not knowing what to do. It's a case of Banquet
Interruptus. All of us gathered together, nobody wants to
go to bed – The mind boggles what people will get up to
now! (*He lowers his voice.*) If you feel like, we could
discuss a little business? . . . Good a time as any –

DANIEL: Not now, Irving –

DANIEL *tries to get away from* IRVING. ALICE *is watching*

97

this, amused.

IRVING (*confidential*): By the way, have you been invited to this country do? (DANIEL *looks blank*) Don't know what I'm talking about, do you?! Martina's engagement party in the country – it's a very select list. I'll see if I can get you an invitation – won't be easy!

DANIEL gets away from IRVING. *He moves over to* ALICE. *Just as he does so, the door of* REBECCA'*s room opens.*
REBECCA *stares for a split second at* ALICE *and* DANIEL.
ALICE *takes a step forward.*

ALICE: Rebecca . . .

REBECCA: Daniel! I hear everything's OK. That's great news, I'm so glad . . .

Come in here . . . come on . . . in here! . . . I've got something I want you to see . . .

She encourages DANIEL *through the door and closes it firmly. We stay on* ALICE *for a moment, staring after her.*

INT. HOTEL. REBECCA'S ROOM
There is music playing. Mess everywhere. Bottles of drink. All over the bed, there are trays of chocolates, petits fours from the banquet. CHARLES *is kneeling on the bed staring through an old stereoscope, battered old binoculars with beautiful period slides.*

REBECCA: Look – Charles has stolen this from Stephen's room.

CHARLES: And it's really rather beautiful . . . Come and have a look . . .

DANIEL kneels by CHARLES *on the bed, looking through the stereoscope. We see slides from the early 1900s, slides of people dressed in fancy dress, especially long-faced and serious people. A plump man is standing in front of a painted backdrop.*

CHARLES (*changing the slides for* DANIEL): That's the
patriarch, Gilbert . . . your great-grandfather.
*We see more slides from the late Edwardian era. A rather
intriguing looking figure, a young woman of about eighteen
with a veil, sitting in profile.*

CHARLES: That's Henrietta . . . my grandmother, the only
one who hasn't dressed up in some ridiculous Ruritanian
peasant costume. They had this compulsion at that time
for putting on awful fancy dress –

REBECCA: It's amazing how you go through a whole series of
faces – and then suddenly one just leaps out at you.
DANIEL *stares at the slide of* HENRIETTA. *The veil, the
figure in profile.*

DANIEL: God, yes, this is a wonderful old thing!
More slides of HENRIETTA *including a portrait of her with
the veil lifted. A slide of her sitting in a luxury Venetian-
looking Edwardian hotel room, with cherubs and angels
decorating the walls. A rich sensual room, with* HENRIETTA
*posed in the middle of it. And then there are more slides of
the fancy-dress party.* DANIEL *is changing the slides himself
now. With the music playing in the room, he is becoming
entranced.*

DANIEL: It's great, almost a 3D effect! Draws you right in
there. (*As he stares through the stereoscope.*) I wonder if
people will be looking at pictures of the banquet tonight
in a hundred years' time?!
DANIEL *looks up, he realises he's been talking to himself,
because* REBECCA *and* CHARLES *are in a corner, sitting
very close together, whispering to each other. He can half
hear what they're saying.*

CHARLES: Why can't we leave now? There's no need to stay
till morning . . . (*Their faces very closely.*) I don't think I
can last till morning –
REBECCA *is talking to him softly.*

REBECCA: We're nearly through . . . it's nearly over.

DANIEL: Shall I go? Is everything OK?

> REBECCA *looks up, she's so deeply concentrating on* CHARLES, *it's like she's forgotten* DANIEL *is there for a moment.*

REBECCA: Oh, Daniel . . . there's no need to go – We've just drunk too much . . . (*softly*) or maybe it's the chocolates . . .

DANIEL (*moving to go*): I think I better . . .

REBECCA (*concentrating on* CHARLES): Come back whenever you like . . .

INT. HOTEL RED PASSAGE. NIGHT.

DANIEL *is looking for his key. Just as he is about to go into his room, he glances up in surprise – his mother is approaching down the red passage.*

DANIEL: Mum?! Is everything all right? I thought you were –

ESTHER (*cutting him off*): I came back because he was fast asleep . . . I'll be there for when he wakes up . . . I came looking for you.

DANIEL: For me?

ESTHER: Is that so strange . . . ? I want you to come with me . . . (*as they move down the passage.*) You never asked me who was on my printout – the person who has requested to see me – and now they want to see you.

INT. HOTEL BEDROOM. NIGHT.

The door opens and we see it is VIOLET *and* EDITH*'s bedroom. The lighting is subdued. There seem to be a lot of boxes piled around the room.* GRACE *is sitting in her usual severe way in the corner. But her sisters smile a very warm welcome.*

100

VIOLET (*to* DANIEL): We so wanted to meet you properly . . .
so wanted to catch up!

DANIEL *is very startled that his mother should want to be
with these women at this particular moment. He sees his
mother kick off her shoes and sit on the floor like a student.*

ESTHER: I thought it would be very interesting for you,
Daniel, to meet Violet, Edith and Grace properly.

VIOLET (*little jolly laugh*): Oh, how can we live up to that?!

ESTHER (*smiles back at* VIOLET): Oh, you can, and more . . .

DANIEL *sits on the corner of the bed, he sees how fascinated
his mother is. She is leaning forward as if her whole body is
gripped by curiosity. It's as if she's getting ready for
something.*

DANIEL*'S attention is then caught by the sight of a large
stack of biscuit tins. They are piled high, almost as if the
sisters are stockpiling provisions.*

EDITH: Oh, yes – would you like a biscuit? We are never
without a good supply as you can see. (*She chuckles and
leans forward with the biscuits.*) Chocolate or ginger?

As DANIEL *takes the biscuit, he sees that the gaunt* GRACE *is
staring straight at him.*

INT. HOTEL DINING ROOM. MORNING.

SIDNEY *and* IRVING *eating full English breakfast, gazing around
at other members of the family also taking breakfast in the
big sleepy dining room.* STEPHEN *eating on his own,
surrounded by a lot of fruit, carefully peeling a pear. The two
sisters chattering away chirpily, as* GRACE *sits quietly
between them. The missing man sitting silently with his wife.*
IRVING *casts a baleful eye over all of them.*

IRVING: Who are we going to see again? Who's got a ticket
for the country event? Who's on the absolute A-list?

MARTINA *arrives, holding a towel, calls over to the whole dining room with great confidence, making both family and non-family members look up.*

MARTINA: Anyone coming for a swim? Come on everyone! Be great to have a lot of you in there with me!

SIDNEY (*muttering*): I wanted to have a go at the family karaoke, there's still a weird sense of things being cut off in the middle . . .

INT. DANIEL'S HOTEL ROOM/PASSAGE. MORNING.
Morning light. DANIEL *lying naked in bed. His eyes half open as he hears his voice being called faintly.*

We cut to him opening the door into the passage with a sheet round him. He sees his mother standing there, all smartly dressed ready to go out.

DANIEL (*rubbing the sleep from his face*): Hi . . . How's Dad?

ESTHER: It's OK, your dad is fine. I've already been there this morning. I was there at six o'clock.

DANIEL: Really?! You can't have slept at all –

ESTHER: Yes, he seems much better. You go to work, and see him this evening.

DANIEL: Right . . . Is he going to agree to the arrangements? Staying up in London?

ESTHER: He's going to have to. It's what's best.

ESTHER *moves off.* DANIEL *watches her go, startled by her decisiveness. The door of the room next to him opens and* REBECCA *is there. She is fully dressed.*

REBECCA: So everything's all right? With your dad?

DANIEL: I think so . . . (*He's standing there naked with the sheet around his waist.*)

REBECCA (*producing a piece of paper*): I was just going to give you this. They are my numbers. (*She hands him the piece of paper.*)

DANIEL: Right . . . Great!

He takes them, there's no obvious place to put them.

REBECCA *smiles watching him move the piece of paper from one hand to another while holding on to the sheet.*

REBECCA (*lightly*): Don't lose them . . .

DANIEL *glances down the passage, at the guests leaving their rooms and porters moving luggage.*

DANIEL: Just when you've started to meet your family, everybody is going home. Seems a pity . . .

REBECCA: It is a pity.

REBECCA *looks at him for a moment.*

DANIEL (*as suavely as he can manage in the circumstances*): Can I invite you in? . . . I'll rustle up some orange juice.

REBECCA *leans forward and gives him a light peck on the cheek.*

REBECCA: Not just now . . .

EXT. INDUSTRIAL BUILDING. MORNING.

DANIEL *arrives driving a small rather battered Toyota, outside a grim-looking empty industrial building. He is greeted by an impatient looking* ANGRY MAN, *who starts shouting as soon as the car stops, even before he has got out.*

ANGRY MAN: Are you the bloody surveyor?

DANIEL: I am the bloody surveyor, I think . . .

ANGRY MAN: I've been waiting for hours to let you in! For crying out loud, aren't any of you guys ever EVER on time!! . . . A punctual surveyor – that'll be the day! The amount of time that all of us who do a proper job waste waiting around for you . . . it's unbelievable . . . billions of pounds go down the pan every year – because of you! I'm going to let you in, and leave you to get the hell on with it

103

– (He's rattling a large bunch of keys as he opens the door.)
As DANIEL *enters the building, the* ANGRY MAN *calls after*
him.
You'll have fun in there! I can tell you!

INT. INDUSTRIAL BUILDING. DAY.
A huge empty area. DANIEL *is alone, right in the middle,*
measuring the great space. He is using a combination of his
electronic distance measure (EDM) and a large tape measure. As
he measures he sees the little prince staring at him. We see the
deep preoccupation in his eyes, he is totally unable to concentrate
on his work. He takes out his phone and dials.

DANIEL (*hearing voicemail*): Rebecca, I'm alone in this huge
        empty building . . . I just thought I'd use one of your
        numbers to see if there's any possibility of seeing you
        again – like tonight, for instance (*he grins*) or even in
        fifty-five minutes? . . .
        He rings off. Kneeling alone in the vast space with tape
        measure. The phone rings almost immediately. He leaps to
        answer it to be greeted by RAYMOND*'s voice.*
RAYMOND: You bastard . . . Do you realise what's happened?
        . . . Do you realise where I've been put?!

INT. MANSION FLAT STAIRS/LANDINGS. LATE
MORNING.
DANIEL *approaches up the stairs of large gloomy London*
mansion flats. The decor is wood-panelling and thick red carpets.
There is quite a grand-looking entrance at the end of the landing.
DANIEL *rings the bell. A* NURSE *opens the door. Her face looks*
rather shocked.
DANIEL: I'm Daniel . . . I think my father is here . . .

The NURSE *looking very grave.*

NURSE: Yes . . .

DANIEL: Has something happened?

Before the NURSE *can reply, we hear* RAYMOND *hoarsely yelling from somewhere deep in the flat.* DANIEL *moves through the sombre flat to find his father sitting up in bed, in a large bedroom overlooking a leafy secretive garden square.*

DANIEL approaches.

RAYMOND: I'll never forgive you . . . ! *Never!* Being stuck here in Ernest's flat, servants, nurses. Absolute nightmare! Why can't I be in my own bed? You all decided I can't and it's complete rubbish!

DANIEL (*smiles*): You sound better . . .

INT. HOTEL RED PASSAGE. AFTERNOON.

REBECCA *is coming out of her hotel room, at the same time that* ALICE *is emerging from her suite at the end of the passage. At the other end of the passage* SIDNEY *is leaving his room, heaving two hefty bags.* REBECCA *catches* ALICE'*s look.* ALICE *seems eager to say something to her, but* REBECCA *manages to deflect the moment by calling after* SIDNEY.

REBECCA: I'll help you with those, Sidney.

SIDNEY: Really! Most kind. (*he smiles.*) I'm too mean to use a porter – then I always regret it!

REBECCA moves off with SIDNEY, *not looking back at* ALICE.

INT. ERNEST'S MANSION FLAT. BEDROOM. AFTERNOON.

RAYMOND *is lying back on his pillows looking defiantly morose.* DANIEL *is standing at the end of the bed watching him. He is still wearing the long leather coat.*

RAYMOND: I want to kill myself . . .

DANIEL: You certainly *are* better.

RAYMOND: Just can't stop thinking about the banquet . . . I can see them all with the food half up to their mouths, frozen in astonishment . . . What's more I'm surrounded by these deadly pictures – (*We see gloomy pictures of gardens.*) Only person who'd be happy here is your mother – with her love of fiddling around in gardens . . .
RAYMOND'*s tone is sharp and light, but there is a sadness in his eyes.*

DANIEL (*smiles*): I could take the pictures down . . .

RAYMOND: I'm meant to be getting better here! But I'm being hammered . . . hammered by really dark thoughts. My health will get worse, bits of my brain are already going, the future looks grim . . .
DANIEL *is unfazed by his father's dark mood.*

DANIEL: I think I can stop you killing yourself.

RAYMOND: How?

DANIEL: By telling you something very surprising.

RAYMOND: Oh yes . . . What about? (*He looks at him.*) Why are you wearing that coat – I thought it was meant to be summer out there?

DANIEL (*taking the leather coat off*): Oh, yes, doesn't quite fit me, does it . . . but there's a story behind this . . .

RAYMOND: You're not going to tell me a story about a coat?! (*Disbelief.*) He is going to try to save me with a coat anecdote!

DANIEL: No, forget the coat. It's something I learned yesterday.

RAYMOND: About whom?

DANIEL: About the old sisters. The two jolly sisters and the tall spooky one.

RAYMOND: Oh, for goodness sake! I thought at least it might be about Alice. There's nothing you could tell me about those sisters that could possibly be of interest.

DANIEL (*calmly*): No. This is good.

RAYMOND: If it's not, you're fired.

DANIEL (*smiles*): Your father's brother Maurice left London and settled in Birmingham in the early thirties.

RAYMOND: Yes, yes, he died before I was born. There's nothing special there.

DANIEL: He was quite a gruff sort of character . . . Like a less confident version of your father – I think, even though he was a lot older . . . same non-conformity, same desire to get away from the family in London . . .

RAYMOND Yes, yes –

DANIEL: They were quite a taciturn sort of couple, Maurice and Ruth.

We see MAURICE *and* RUTH *sitting in a modest sitting room, viewed from a child's point of view through banisters.* MAURICE *cursing and making a mess of trying to light the fire.*

DANIEL: They were a strangely clumsy pair, and not good at arranging their lives. Even the simplest things became quite complicated. But they had their three children. The two little ones, Violet and Edith –

We see the two little girls peering through the banisters at the mess around the fire, as MAURICE *struggles to get it lit.*

DANIEL: And this glorious daughter, the older one, Grace.

We cut back to RAYMOND.

RAYMOND: She was glorious? I doubt that very much. How do you know she was glorious?

We see this tall beautiful young woman of seventeen, brushing the two smaller girls' hair and getting them ready to go out.

DANIEL (*VO*): The little ones called her Mary Grace, because when Violet was very small the first time she said her name, she was trying to say 'My Grace' but it sounded

107

like Mary Grace, so that's what she was called.

We cut back to RAYMOND *rolling his eyes at this.* DANIEL *forges ahead.*

DANIEL (*VO*): And Mary Grace was fantastically good at everything. She managed the house, she ordered things for her parents . . .

MARY GRACE *decorates* VIOLET *and* EDITH*'s bedroom with a very well-drawn mural, the smaller girls are helping her.*

DANIEL (*VO*): And the two little ones worshipped her . . . She told them stories, she drew elaborate pictures up on their walls, their love for her was exceptionally strong . . . She was their whole world . . .

RAYMOND: So she ran the house!

DANIEL: The war comes and the two little ones are evacuated out of Birmingham to North Wales.

RAYMOND: Oh please, not a story of them being tortured by a frightful couple who took them in.

DANIEL: No, not quite.

We see a group of children being lined up in a cinema in front of the blank screen, wearing cards with their names on them round their necks. In the first few rows of the auditorium local couples sit inspecting the children, selecting them. We see another image, this time a still, of evacuated children in cattle pens as local people inspect them.

The flashback unfolds mainly in live action, but it is punctuated by stills.

We return to the cinema, in live action, a dour-looking couple watching the two little sisters.

DANIEL: The pair that chose them.

The elderly couple examine the cards round the children's neck cautiously, and then indicate that these are the two children they have chosen.

DANIEL: The couple were a bit severe . . . And the children found them quite sinister.

We see the woman of the household staring at the children in their bedroom through a crack in the door. The children staring back, clearly terrified.

DANIEL: They didn't torture or abuse the children. But what the two little girls had to do – was an awful lot of cleaning.

We see the two sisters scrubbing the kitchen floor.

RAYMOND: I bet they were good at that, Violet and Edith, always so rosy-cheeked.

DANIEL: Nothing horrible happened –

RAYMOND: Blimey – this isn't just them stuck in a gloomy Welsh household?! . . . You've had your chance, you're fired.

DANIEL (*defiant*): Oh no, not yet. The two little sisters desperately missed their Mary Grace.

A shot of the beautiful MARY GRACE.

DANIEL: Just before they had been evacuated, she'd been courted by a handsome young officer, an RAF office called William.

We see images of the young couple together, both photos and live action. They are moving a long a wall in a park, blurred figures passing either side of them.

DANIEL: It made Violet and Edith all the more eager to see her. So they decided to walk home.

We see the two children set off down a long straight road. The image of their walk down this road keeps recurring.

DANIEL: There were very few vehicles allowed on the road of course . . . except for military vehicles.

We see an armoured car rolling past them, as the two girls walk down the long straight road.

RAYMOND: They walked home from North Wales to Birmingham! I don't believe a word of it, they would have been picked up within hours –

We see the armoured car stopping and turning. It waits for

the girls way ahead of them on the road, as they walk
towards it.

DANIEL: They were good at explaining if they were stopped
by any adult, that they belonged to that farm across the
hedge and they had just been sent on an errand . . . At
night they kept out of the way . . .

We see headlights of a military convoy stabbing along the
road.

DANIEL (*VO*): Except one night they saw a truly
extraordinary thing.

We see the children staring through a gate down into a field
full of military personnel who are patrolling with powerful
torches. The lights criss-crossing all over the field.

As we get closer, we see the military unit is collecting cobwebs
and putting them in secure containers.

DANIEL: Armed soldiers collecting cobwebs, because of the
scare that was happening then – that these apparent
cobwebs might be some form of German chemical
warfare, because there had been an usually high number
of cobwebs that summer in England.

It was an official nationwide scare. But secret.

RAYMOND's *eyebrow is raised in disbelief.*

RAYMOND: Never heard that . . . You mean the army went
around collecting cobwebs at night to help beat the
Germans! And the girls saw that . . . ?

We see the children's faces, framed by a cobweb, staring at
this military operation. The adult world solemnly collecting
cobwebs.

RAYMOND: They must have thought everybody had gone
crazy!

The images of the walk intensify. The little legs and the long
straight road. Their clothes becoming progressively dirtier.

We see them from behind, moving down the empty road, like
the Start Rite shoe poster of the sixties and seventies.

DANIEL: They reach their home and even your surly uncle and my surly great-uncle gives them a welcome.

We seen an awkward and stilted reunion, MAURICE *and* RUTH *kissing the tops of their heads. Following this, the two adults start wandering in bemused circles in their sitting room.*

DANIEL: And they even remember to inform the authorities . . .

But there is an even greater abstracted air about the household. There is no mention of Mary, Mary Grace . . . And when they run up the stairs to see her, her door is locked. She refuses to open it for a while.

DANIEL *catches his father's eye.* RAYMOND *is becoming deeply interested despite himself.*

DANIEL: And the parents are living in this filthy house . . . with unwashed clothes and dust. The place has become squalid.

We see the thick grease in the kitchen and the murals in the bedroom that MARY GRACE *drew have become stained and filthy.*

DANIEL (*VO*): When they eventually get Mary Grace to open the door, her room is even more shocking, there are layers of dust and dirt and grease . . . it looks like the sheets haven't been changed for months and the walls are blackened with cigarette smoke.

MARY GRACE *is curled in a ball. The two little sisters stare at her, uncertain what to do. We cut back to* RAYMOND.

RAYMOND: Her lover is dead!

DANIEL: Her lover is missing . . . and she has gone into a state of grief . . . her whole body and mind consumed. She has blotted out everything except her grief. Her whole system seems to have shut down. And for Violet and Edith there seems not a trace left of their glorious sister. The little ones start cleaning.

We see the two girls transforming the kitchen very professionally. A high shot of MAURICE *wandering in circles between them as they scrub.*

DANIEL: The atmosphere is rather hellish, the parents walking about like zombies . . . so reliant on their older daughter – now she's locked herself away, nothing works. And Maurice is given to outbursts of temper and floods of irascible and slightly surreal tirades . . .

RAYMOND: Yes, yes! I get the reference . . . Get on with it!

DANIEL: One day Mary Grace goes off into town, finally to do some shopping.

We see MARY GRACE, *her gaunt straight posture now discernible, standing at the top of the stairs, having at last changed her clothes. But she moves past the two little girls without even looking at them.*

DANIEL: But she barely acknowledges them. So Violet and Edith decide to set off again, maybe to head for London this time because they know they have family there. And maybe a better family –

RAYMOND: Could hardly be worse –

DANIEL: They are also grieving for a sister who is no longer their sister . . .

They only walk a very few miles that first day. They begin to have second thoughts . . .

We seen them in a wide shot going up a steep field.

DANIEL: And they lie down in a wood for the night.

We see their faces framed by branches.

DANIEL: Way, way in the distance they can hear the heavy drone of bombers . . .

Through the wood's canopy we see the two figures of the girls lying close, and the distant sound of the bombers.

DANIEL: It's one of the worst raids on Birmingham . . .

We see stills of the devastation of Birmingham.

DANIEL: Their parents' house takes a direct hit . . .

A decimated house, period photos including close-up details of bodies buried in the rubble.

RAYMOND: Of course, yes, yes I knew they'd died in the war. I never heard anything about the girls though.

DANIEL: Mary Grace is caught in the centre of the town by the raid, spending the night in a shelter. When she gets back the house is just a hole in the ground. Rubble and bits of bodies . . .

We see even closer details of the photos of rubble. They merge into each other.

DANIEL: And it is presumed somewhere in there, in the ruins, are the little ones.

RAYMOND: But clearly they weren't!

We see the two girls standing on the edge of a wood, staring across a valley.

DANIEL: In the way that children's minds work . . . they think we're here and no one's come after us.

They don't put the sound of the bombs and the possible destruction of their home together because they're thinking that everyone should be wondering where they are – but because the parents and Mary Grace are so caught up in their own world, nobody's bothered to come and look . . .

So they stay in the wood the next day to see what happens, and still nobody comes for them . . .

We see the children getting deeper and deeper into the wood.

DANIEL: And somehow it turns into weeks, and then into months –

RAYMOND *is sitting bolt upright in bed.*

RAYMOND: You're telling me that Violet and Edith lived in the woods during the war . . . as some sort of wild children?!

DANIEL: That is what happened. That's what they told me last night.

RAYMOND: I do *not* believe that.

DANIEL: They stole food from farms –

RAYMOND (*very animated*): No, no, I can't accept this – I'm calling a halt now, that's enough. This is fantasy!

DANIEL stares straight at him, seeing how far his father has become engaged.

DANIEL: They raided a network of farms . . . they gradually became experts at rooting around the countryside. They knew where food was being stockpiled . . .

Over the next piece of the story we see a mixture of flashback live action and images of VIOLET, EDITH *and* GRACE *as they are now. Shots of them turning with their box of chocolates during the slide show, of them in their evening dresses chatting away while helping themselves to great spoonfuls of meringue during the buffet, opening their hotel bedroom door to* DANIEL *and beaming at him. And then their younger selves, as wild children, dashing through the wood.*

DANIEL: They stole clothes from washing lines.

We see the little girls wearing a weird mixture of stolen clothes, ill-matching shoes and odd dresses.

DANIEL: In the winter they found a little old Victorian canal building, long disused . . .

We see the children lying in the dark. Through a crack in the wall they can see the water and the dark shape of a passing barge with military personnel on board, bristling with guns.

DANIEL: Occasionally they heard barges full of munitions going past them really close.

In midwinter they were sometimes near starving . . .

We move off DANIEL*'s face telling the story to the pile of biscuit tins the sisters have in their present-day hotel room.*

VIOLET*'s head turns, as she is now, smiling her rosy-cheeked smile. And* EDITH *offers a biscuit.*

DANIEL: And sometimes a dark piece of the war came very close.

We see through thick summer foliage the two girls watching a military staff car snaking through the outskirts of the wood. The driver, wearing a senior officer's insignia, gets out of the car, the girls watching from a distance. The officer moves to the boot of the car and takes out a bundle, what looks like a woman's body wrapped in a sheet. He begins to bury it.

The girls charge off through the woods, fleeing for their lives.

DANIEL: They even inspired a search party to go hunting, because local farmers thought they were having so much food stolen, there must be a German airman surviving in the woods . . .

We see the girls now with fierce experienced faces, dodging through the trees, as across the rim of the wood a search party is hunting with dogs.

RAYMOND: You're not claiming that they were in the woods for the whole war, like the Japanese who came fighting out of the undergrowth because they thought the war was still on! (*He laughs.*) Violet and Edith?! –

DANIEL: No, finally their luck ran out.

The two little girls come upon a picnic of two soldiers and two girls. They look now thoroughly undomesticated, tough wild children.

DANIEL: It was the women who didn't believe them . . .

We see the women staring into the children's eyes.

RAYMOND *has got out of bed. He is becoming thoroughly animated.*

RAYMOND: This is wonderful twaddle! – I can just about believe their walk – but the idea of them living in the woods! It must be rubbish – but in a way it's almost as good that they have invented all this, that they wanted such a romantic story to be part of their lives! And who would have thought that old boot Grace had such passion . . .

115

We see GRACE, *as she is now, in her evening dress for the banquet, sitting on her own in the passage. Stern and unyielding.*

DANIEL (*thrilled at the effect he has hard on his father*): Their reunion must have been weird, mustn't it . . . ?!

We see the two sisters, now dressed in school uniform, approaching GRACE *across a big room.* GRACE *is sitting very far away, very straight on a high-backed chair. This is followed by the image of them in a strange cluster,* GRACE *in the middle, the two sisters holding her close.* GRACE'*s face is quietly grave.* EDITH *presses her face into the tall, gaunt figure of* GRACE.

EDITH: We'll go to London – the family there will see to us . . .

We cut back to DANIEL.

DANIEL: The best bit for me is the sisters being taken to the studio for those pictures! All got up for the season after the war . . .

And yet underneath all the deb stuff there are these wild children lurking, just barely repressed below the surface, staring at all these upper-class girls.

A flashback of debutante girls making a deafening noise, giggling and poking fun at the two ungainly sisters as they try and pull up their dresses a little bit. They move with painful difficulty in their dainty shoes. We see a montage of society photos of the time interrupting the live action, then we return to the ruthless gaze of the two young sisters, as they watch the gathering of debs.

RAYMOND: There were those boots, weren't there . . . ?! Those strange hobo boots in their picture . . . their society photo . . .

DANIEL: That's right!

We see images of the little legs walking and walking.

RAYMOND: You don't mean to say you believe them?!

116

DANIEL: Oh yes . . . I think it's true. A great story of sibling love – And rejection by your parents, and by your elder sister . . .

A spiral of images of the little girls and the old women.
RAYMOND *is completely energised by this story despite expressing total disbelief.*

RAYMOND: Children did live wild during the evacuation . . . they roamed the streets in a few places and stole things . . . But *not* Violet and Edith . . . !

An amazing idea (*He laughs.*) An amazing and beautiful idea . . . (*He grins.*) And it's so typical of my father that he never said anything about this . . . And of course their weird relationship now . . .

We see the two sisters propping up the tall GRACE *between them, walking slowly down the hotel passage.*

RAYMOND: Come on, you bastard, let's have lunch!

INT. HOTEL GROUND-FLOOR PASSAGES/POPPY'S OFFICE. DAY.
ESTHER *knocks on the door and pushes it open. She is holding her laptop and a big folder.* STEPHEN *is sitting in the middle of* POPPY's *office surrounded by all the paper and the large family tree behind his head.* ESTHER *stands in the doorway.*

STEPHEN: Hello, I thought you'd left. Raymond? Is he . . . ?
ESTHER: He is being an encouragingly bad patient. I just wondered if you had a moment . . .
STEPHEN: Well, it depends for what – I'm actually in the middle of researching something –
ESTHER: I just wanted to see if you had time to glance through these . . .

She approaches his desk.

ESTHER: I've been e-mailing and using the Internet, the

international genealogy site, both before I came here and again lots while I've been here (*smiles*), inspired by your talk –

STEPHEN: And you've collected your results . . .

ESTHER *has put her laptop down and is turning it on.*

ESTHER: Yes. My family name is Dent, which is fairly common, I suppose, but not *that* common, which helps and I just wanted your opinion on how to sift through these for the ones that might be the real thing . . .

STEPHEN: Sift? Well, yes, maybe (*smiles*), I find it hard to resist a good sift. I have not often been known to say no. (*He looks at her.*) What are you looking for? Anything particular . . . ? Or should I say what are you hoping for?

ESTHER: Well, naturally some interesting connection . . . not necessarily something incredible, some famous relation, that's pretty rare, I expect . . . I know that I'm not putting this very well . . . but anything that might set something off in my mind (*she smiles, embarrassed*), so to speak.

INT. ERNEST'S MANSION FLAT. DINING ROOM. AFTERNOON.

RAYMOND and DANIEL *at either end of a long table in the dining room of the wood-panelled mansion flat. The* NURSE *is sitting in the corner, watching. Bowls of soup in front of them.*

RAYMOND: I've never seen the point of soup.

NURSE: I'm sorry, it's the doctor's orders.

DANIEL: It's fine. We'll *all* just eat soup.

RAYMOND: It's *not* fine. A diet of gruel while I'm forced to stay in Ernest's bloody gloomy flat! It's recipe for disaster.

DANIEL (*smiles down the table*): It's quite funny –

RAYMOND: What?

DANIEL: You ending up here – Everything you hate . . .
    surrounded by Ernest's things . . .

RAYMOND (*grunts at this and then glances round*): It is very
    bizarre, the décor – but he does have, strangely enough,
    a rather interesting collection of videos, all these old
    British films . . . I remember them from my youth . . .
    Jack Hawkins in –
    There is a small knock on the dining-room door and
    REBECCA *is standing there with a large bunch of flowers,*
    being escorted by the maid.

REBECCA: Ah! I'm so glad to see you up and about . . .
    She moves into the room

RAYMOND: Yes. I'm in fighting mood . . .

REBECCA (*moving to the end of the table next to* DANIEL): So I
    hear, from all the messages left for me by your son. I
    brought you these . . .

RAYMOND: Thank you. Most kind. Can I interest you in
    some very murky vegetable soup.

REBECCA: That's a very tempting offer – but I think I'll just
    get these into water . . . (*She looks straight at* DANIEL.)

INT. ERNEST'S MANSION FLAT. KITCHEN. AFTERNOON.
REBECCA *is standing in the kitchen with her back to us finding a*
vase for the flowers, and then arranging them in the vase.
DANIEL *comes into the kitchen.*

REBECCA: He seems much better.

DANIEL: He is.

REBECCA (*arranging the flowers*): Can I trust you, Daniel?

DANIEL (*surprised*): Trust me? (*Lightly.*) That sounds
    promising. (*Staring at her.*) Of course.

REBECCA: This will seem a rather unconventional request . . .

but I want you to take a message for me.

DANIEL: Take a message? Where to?

REBECCA: Just back to the hotel.

DANIEL: Right . . . You can't fax it?

REBECCA: It's a verbal message.

DANIEL: I see. Sorry to be so plodding, but why not use the phone?

REBECCA: Because this is how it has to be delivered. It has to be done by somebody else.

DANIEL: And who's the message for?

REBECCA: It's for Alice. (*Watching him.*) You don't look surprised –

DANIEL: I had no idea who you were going to say . . . not a clue. What is the message?

REBECCA: It is simply to tell her, 'What you're asking is not possible. There's no way that can happen.'

That's the message.

DANIEL: Are you going to write that down for me?

REBECCA: No, I'm sure you can remember it, Daniel.

DANIEL: Right –

REBECCA: There's something else. I want you to describe to me exactly Alice's response when you give her the message. How she looks, what happens . . .

(*She smiles.*) I told you it was an unconventional request.

DANIEL: And I suppose you're not going to tell me why you can't do it yourself?

REBECCA: Let's just say it's complicated and embarrassing.

Alice and I are not talking.

That's why I need you. I know it seems weird . . . But actually it's not that strange . . .

DANIEL: It *is* strange.

REBECCA: You won't do it?

DANIEL (*watching her closely*): Of course I will.

120

REBECCA (*softly*): Thank you. (*Efficient.*) She'll be in her suite
　　between six and seven tonight. Don't ring her before.
　　Just go and do it.
DANIEL: Just appear?
REBECCA: And here's the trust part – you mustn't tell anyone.
　　Nobody. Especially not Charles. I don't want to know
　　what you're doing. (*Firmly.*) Understand?

EXT. HOTEL. EARLY EVENING.
DANIEL *approaches the hotel, he is still wearing the leather coat.*
Just as he is about to enter the hotel, he sees the three sisters,
VIOLET, EDITH *and* GRACE, *walking along the street together,*
each carrying shopping bags. The tall GRACE *in the middle. They*
are moving slowly together, glancing into the shop windows.

INT. HOTEL FOYER/ORIENTAL BAR. EARLY EVENING.
DANIEL *walks through the hotel lobby, the coat is too long for him*
and is brushing the carpet. A voice calls his name. DANIEL *turns*
to see IRVING *and* SIDNEY *sitting in the Oriental Bar surrounded*
by very decorative wallpaper of exotic birds. The early-evening
sun is giving the walls a rich red hue. SIDNEY *has his bags*
heaped next to him on a chair.

IRVING: Daniel! My useful cousin! Come and join us!
　　DANIEL *approaches them, the two fleshy men, surrounded*
　　by this most delicate of décor.
IRVING: We're just having a farewell drink in these delightful
　　surroundings . . .
DANIEL: I can't stay.
IRVING: He's always got an appointment!
DANIEL: No, I'm just acting as a – (*He stops himself.*) I've just
　　got to make one very quick call.

121

SIDNEY: I like your coat.

IRVING: Well, if you can't join us now, then you must come back, can't let you go before doing business. I need to appraise you of the full operation. I have my own international network – he looks surprised, yes, fully transglobal. I may be in Japan later this week or it could be Darlington!

I have information about properties, what properties are up for sale all over the world . . . furthermore I have my own scouts on the ground, smelling out their true condition – could be an opening for you there.

SIDNEY: He's always on the move.

IRVING: While *he* never moves out of Shepherd's Bush. Not if he can help it!

SIDNEY: That's right. Sedentary Sidney . . .

DANIEL (*trying to get away*): I mustn't be late. So –

IRVING: Mustn't miss his call! (*He leans forward towards* DANIEL, *indicating* SIDNEY.) You and him have a lot in common, you know . . .

DANIEL (*startled*): Really?

SIDNEY: Could be . . .

IRVING: Same interest in many ways . . . must be in the genes! First man to introduce road humps to London – Sidney was. Oh yes! Road planner extraordinaire . . . the Napoleon III of inner London.

SIDNEY (*sipping drink*): Hidden talents, very well hidden, but they're there somewhere.

IRVING*'s mobile phone rings.*

IRVING (*as he reaches in his pocket to get it*): Is this Tokyo or is this Darlington?! (*He answers and* looks up at DANIEL.) It's Darlington.

DANIEL *is moving off.*

IRVING: Don't forget to return for the offer you will not be able to refuse!

122

Raymond making his speech at the banquet.

Raymond's dancing father.

Daniel as the little prince.

The garden of the stone beasts.

Henrietta watching from the trees.

Richard, the missing brother, during his happy childhood.

Richard during his illness.

Rebecca watches Daniel wake from his dream in the Foreign Office.

Daniel with his cousin Rebecca.

The picture that Daniel finds of Alice in the London house.

Charles, Alice and Rebecca about to abandon Richard in the woods.

Edith and Violet, the wild children, all dressed up after the war.

(*Watching* DANIEL go.) There's nothing like having a surveyor in the family . . .

INT. HOTEL RED PASSAGE. EVENING.
DANIEL *walks towards* ALICE'*s suite which is at the end of the red passage. As he moves down the passage, he hears some powerful, intense music coming out of another room. He can't resist moving towards the door of the room which is half open. He sees* CHARLES *sitting in* STEPHEN'*s room, bending over* STEPHEN'*s computer. There is a half-empty bottle of whiskey next to the computer and a glass.* CHARLES *empties the glass.*

CHARLES: Hi.
DANIEL: Charles . . .
There are papers spread all over STEPHEN'*s room, as if they have been rifled, files lying open everywhere.*
CHARLES: I'm just breaking into Stephen's computer.
DANIEL: So I see . . .
CHARLES: Don't close the door . . . ! If Stephen appears I want him to see what I'm doing.
He types, accessing another file in the computer.
CHARLES: What are you doing here again, Daniel?
DANIEL: I'm doing someone a favour . . . (*He stops, decides not to say any more.*)
CHARLES: Who might that be?
DANIEL (*slight grin*): You know . . . just family business.
CHARLES *pours him a large tumbler of whiskey.*
CHARLES: Come on. You can keep me company. (*With surprising force.*) And take that coat off!
DANIEL *takes the coat off.* CHARLES'*s mood is very concentrated and intense. He thrust the whiskey into* DANIEL'*s hand.*
DANIEL: I oughtn't to . . . I haven't really slept properly for

123

two days – I'm a little stoned from lack of sleep. (*Nevertheless he takes a big swig of whiskey.*) I ran into Irving downstairs. You're right. He's got round to it, he's about to offer me a job!

CHARLES: I'll show you what you can do with Stephen's machine . . . (*He is tapping in* IRVING*'s name.*) There he is . . . (*A picture of* IRVING *as he is now comes up on screen.*) Now watch this – there is fleshly old Irving but look at some of the people he's descended from . . . his grandmother, her sister, and his mother . . .

These fragile beautiful women appear on the screen.

CHARLES: All these glorious delicate creatures . . . begetting Irving.

DANIEL: If you look at him carefully – I suppose in a funny way he is rather beautiful . . .

CHARLES (*drinking, whiskey, rifling through more papers*): You know historically our society is far more mobile than people think . . . Taxi drivers turn out to have dukes in their family . . . unlike some European countries where the aristocracy never bred with anyone else. Now, Daniel. (*Taps at the computer.*) Anybody that you want, fire away, let's see what Stephen's got on them! Who will it be?

DANIEL *hesitates for a moment.*

DANIEL: Grace, Mary Grace.

CHARLES: Really? Are you sure?

DANIEL: I'm sure.

CHARLES (*tapping in* GRACE): She's not called Mary Grace. *This amazing picture of* GRACE *appears, a studio society photo just after the war, a very romantic picture. But there is already the intense faraway obsessive look in her eyes.*

CHARLES: That's a surprise. What a great picture! Who would have thought she once looked like that! (*He starts to fill up* DANIEL*'s glass with more whisky, while staring at* GRACE*'s picture.*)

CHARLES: You know the Japanese Buddhists keep a
permanent altar to their ancestors in their house the
whole time . . . a tablet with carved names on it . . .
(*Drinking.*) What'd happen, do you think, if we did the
same . . . ?

DANIEL (*putting the full tumbler of whiskey down*): No. I'm not
having any more. I've got to go.

CHARLES (*his manner progressively more volatile, drunk*): No,
you've got to see this. Want to show you (*He produces an
image of the family tree on the computer.*) Stephen did lots
of different designs and drafts of the tree, he
experimented with all sorts of different layouts . . . (*He
has printed out a lot of the drafts, they surround the
computer.*) You see, he had so many goes at it . . .
CHARLES *scrunches up one of these drafts and flicks it across
the room as he says the line.* DANIEL *is surprised by*
CHARLES*'s venom.* DANIEL *has also picked up one of the
drafts of the family tree in an absent-minded sort of way.*

DANIEL: Yes, he's such a perfectionist. (*He puts the draft in
his pocket.*) I have an appointment – I really do have to
go.
DANIEL *moves to the door.* CHARLES *is staring at the
computer.*

CHARLES (*with fierce authority*): Keep the door open.
DANIEL *is instinctively closing it behind him.*

CHARLES: No, no, further than that – open it.
DANIEL *moves down the passage towards* ALICE*'s suite. He
is acutely conscious of* CHARLES *working at the computer
through the open door. If* CHARLES *happens to look up he
can see* DANIEL *waiting outside* ALICE*'s door.*
DANIEL *knocks.*

DANIEL (*murmurs*): I left the coat . . .
In the pause as he stands outside ALICE*'s door, he is
watching very keenly to see if* CHARLES *looks up.*

INT. ALICE'S SUITE/PASSAGE. EVENING.

ALICE *opens the door. A very momentary flick of surprise to see* DANIEL *standing there.* DANIEL *tries to be nonchalant.*

DANIEL: Hello, Alice.

ALICE: Daniel . . . that's a nice surprise.

> DANIEL *walks into the suite. It is rather dark in* ALICE'S *part of the suite. In the distance he can see the doors opening to* ERNEST'S *suite which is far more brightly lit. People are moving in the depth of field:* MARTINA *and* NAZIK *are talking French to each other,* ERNEST *is bumbling around dressed for going out to dinner.*

ALICE: We always seem to meet when I'm getting ready . . . We're all just about to go out for a meal in a restaurant Martina has found. You should have let me know you were coming, I would have suggested a little earlier –

DANIEL: Yes . . . I just happened to be in the hotel, and I thought . . .

> *His voice tails off, he's staring at* ALICE. *She looks very elegant.* DANIEL *suddenly finds himself getting nervous.*

ALICE: So you thought you'd drop by? . . . And your father, how is he?

DANIEL: He's very much better –

ALICE: And he's all right in the flat?

DANIEL: Yes . . . I think he's rather enjoying it now – through gritted teeth.

> *He can see* MARTINA *and* NAZIK *having some sort of vigorous discussion in French in the far distance. Their voices ringing out loudly. It's not as private as* DANIEL *had hoped.* DANIEL *decides to take the plunge.*

DANIEL: I'm here for what might seem a rather odd reason . . .

> ALICE *turns.*

ALICE: Which is?

> DANIEL *hesitates.*

126

ALICE: Daniel, you can't start a sentence like that and then not finish it.

DANIEL: Yes . . . (*He swallows.*) I mean, no . . .

> ALICE *moves slightly so that her face is in shadow.* DANIEL *moves, so that he can see her face clearly.*

DANIEL: I have a message for you from Rebecca . . .

ALICE: A message?

> ERNEST *is calling from depth of field, criss-crossing his suite.*

ERNEST: You know, Alice, I still can't find it . . .

ALICE (*calling*): Forget about it, Ernest! . . .

ERNEST: No, no. (*He comes into the mouth of the adjoining doors.*) Stephen found it and handed it to me right here and said give that to Alice, and I put it down for a moment – (*He sees* DANIEL *and acknowledges him.*) Hello, how are you? (*and without waiting for a reply*) I put it down for a moment and it's gone! It was a marvellous thing too . . .

ALICE: It can wait, Ernest – it really doesn't matter. (ALICE *glances at* DANIEL.)

ERNEST: Oh, but it does matter – if I leave it now I'll forget all about it . . . it was a splendid bit of paper . . .

DANIEL: Can I help look? What is it?

ALICE: No. It's a silly thing that Stephen unearthed, he keeps producing the most surprising things – it's from when I was a very young woman and working in advertising . . .

DANIEL (*startled*): Advertising! . . . I would never have guessed, Alice . . . that's the last sort of thing I thought you would have done.

ALICE: Oh yes, I did a whole campaign for milk! It was rather charming and foolish and suddenly it was everywhere. This is so many years ago, before you were born – a huge milk bottle . . . on wheels like a cannon, besieging a town full of coughs and sneezes and germs.

> (*She laughs.*) We were trying to make milk dangerous!

127

And masculine.

ALICE is beginning to doodle on the hotel notepaper, drawing the milk bottle like a cannon besieging a castle wall. As she does so, her voice soft:

ALICE: Go on, Daniel, give the message.

ERNEST has retreated back into his suite and is still searching, muttering, 'It just doesn't seem to be around.' MARTINA is calling in French, 'The car is waiting.' DANIEL is watching ALICE's doodle take shape on the page. He blinks hard.

ALICE: Are you all right?

DANIEL: Yes . . . I've just had rather a lot of whisky. (*He leans closer.*) Rebecca said, 'What you asked is not possible – there's no way it can happen,' . . . or maybe it was the other way round, 'No way it can happen, what you want isn't possible.' . . .

A momentary pause.

ALICE (*staring straight at him*): And?

DANIEL: There isn't an and . . .

ERNEST (*calling in background*): We must go now, Alice . . . My daughter is starving!

MARTINA (*merrily calling*): And when that happens nobody is safe!

ALICE I'll be right down . . . I'll catch you up . . .

MARTINA and NAZIK argue in French. There's a great commotion as they begin to leave in the depth of field. ALICE, in the foreground, leans towards DANIEL.

ALICE: *And*, Daniel? . . . Tell me what else she said.

DANIEL (*hesitates for a second*): I was to watch exactly how you received the message, how you reacted and then tell her.

ALICE: And what will you tell her?

DANIEL (*very slight pause*): That you minded a lot . . .

There is a pause. DANIEL stares at ALICE.

ALICE: Will you take a message back from me? When you see her?

DANIEL: A message back?! You mean, become a go-between? I don't know . . . not without knowing more . . . (*His voice slurs as he begins to feel the effect of the whisky.*) Like why two such amazing women are not talking to each other?

ALICE *watches him.*

DANIEL: Right now . . . (*he's leaning forward as if about to throw up, struggling to control.*) Right at this moment, I have this terrible fear that I'm going to throw up all over this room, Alice. And I would really like to avoid that – if I possible can. First my father, then me – it wouldn't make for a great showing by the Hillingdon contingent . . .

ALICE *lifts up his head.* DANIEL *feels comforted by the physical contact,* ALICE*'s maternal warmth, her elegance.*

ALICE: Don't worry, that wouldn't be the end of the world. We have two huge bathrooms here anyway.

DANIEL *gets up to move to one of them,* ALICE *smiles.*

ALICE: But maybe it would be best if you used Ernest's . . .

We cut to the bathroom. DANIEL *splashing water vigorously on his face. He is surrounded by some really beautiful towels and all* ERNEST*'s various bottles of potions and aftershave. And pinned up next to the mirror in the bathroom, the family tree.*

DANIEL (*murmuring*): They've relegated theirs to the bathroom . . .

He casually pulls out the crumpled draft that he had taken from STEPHEN*'s room. He lifts up rather unsteadily to make a comparison.*

DANIEL: Not that much difference . . . he's just squeezed it . . .

He is just about to put the draft family tree in his pocket when he realises something and he presses the draft hard up against the mirror. He is completely galvanised.

The camera moves along the finished family tree to discover CHARLES *and* REBECCA *clearly marked with their date of birth. Then the camera moves across to the draft family tree, and we see between* CHARLES *and* REBECCA *is another name, another sibling,* RICHARD. *The missing brother. With the date of his birth, 1966. And in an intense close-up we see the date of his death, 1997.*

We move in on DANIEL'*s face, and then back in huge close-up we see the three names,* CHARLES, RICHARD, REBECCA, *side by side.*

DANIEL *sits on the edge of the bath and stares across at the two family trees and the image of himself in the mirror. Some music is coming from* ALICE'*s suite.* DANIEL *becomes aware she is calling.*

ALICE: Are you all right, Daniel?

DANIEL comes out of the bathroom. He sees ALICE *through the double doors, dividing the suites. She's right at the other end of the suite. He approaches her. She looks up, seeing the change in his manner.*

DANIEL: What happened to Richard . . . ?

Momentary pause.

ALICE: He's dead.

DANIEL: Yes, I saw . . . Why? What happened to him?

ALICE: He was killed. He died in an accident.

DANIEL: Nobody told me they had a brother – this whole time, nobody told me what happened.

ALICE (*camly*): We've only known you a few days, Daniel, only been with you for a few hours really . . . Think about it . . . it's not the first thing you come out with when you meet a new relation.

DANIEL moves through the suite to the photo of the three children.

DANIEL: Of course there were three of them.

We see the picture of the three children sitting on a giant tree trunk, laughing together.

DANIEL: I always felt something, you know – like there was a space there, around them. Something incomplete when

130

you saw them – I sensed something . . . (*He murmurs
again.*) Of course there were three of them. (*And then to*
ALICE *as he stares at the children on the tree trunk.*) These
are them? Must be!

ALICE: Yes.

*The children are very close together on the tree trunk, the
young* RICHARD *staring out, seemingly the most animated of
the three. His face is turned joyfully towards the camera.*

ALICE *is standing next to* DANIEL *looking at the picture.*

DANIEL: You've got some more pictures? I want to see him
grown up . . .

You carry the pictures with you? Don't you?

ALICE (*moving over to a drawer*): A few . . .

DANIEL (*following her*): I knew you would have them with
you . . .

We see the first picture. RICHARD, CHARLES *and*
REBECCA. *The two boys in school uniform.* ALICE*'s
collection of family snaps of the children unfolds in front of
us. The children are always photographed together, playing,
studying, tangled up in play-fights, or lying languidly in the
grass.*

ALICE (*as the pictures pass in front of us*): My husband's
brother, their father Louis, bought a house near us in
Buckinghamshire.

They were away a lot, Louis and Margaret, always
abroad . . .

So I saw a great deal of the children – I used to have
them at weekends when they were at their respective
boarding schools, and they came to stay a lot in the
holidays.

Because we had no children, it was easy for us . . .

Pictures of RICHARD *growing up, reaching his teens.*

DANIEL: You were a great surrogate mother, I'm sure . . .

ALICE: I don't know how you can be certain of that, Daniel.

131

DANIEL: Of course I know that, anybody could tell that . . .

The phone rings. ALICE *answers.*

ALICE: Yes, Ernest . . . I just got delayed . . . a call came through for me . . . You go ahead to the restaurant. I've just got to do a couple more things . . . (*Then firmly.*) No, you go ahead now, it's not worth waiting, I'll see you there.

As she is saying this, she pushes the next picture towards DANIEL. *It is the first photograph of* RICHARD *alone. It is of* RICHARD, *aged about twenty, in the long leather coat that* DANIEL *has been wearing, walking along a street, smoking. An image of total confidence and great style.*

DANIEL *flinches at the sight of the coat.*

DANIEL: He *does* look a bit like me . . .

ALICE: A little.

DANIEL: What happened? . . . How did the accident happen?

ALICE: He was rather drunk, he'd gone to a party in the country, he wandered away from the party on to a railway line. He was hit by an Intercity train.

The confident figure stares back at DANIEL. *Their faces exchange looks.*

DANIEL: Hit by a train?! That's terrible.

ALICE: Yes, sudden death is always awful . . . no warning. The voice on the phone letting you know and you're just too shocked to take it in.

(*She stares at the picture with love.*) He was a very interesting, very intelligent young man . . .

ALICE *puts a last picture down of* RICHARD.

He is photographed in his flat, looking relaxed, glamorous, a bit mysterious. Just a hint of a smile. He is surrounded by an interesting eclectic mixture of objects dating from the fifties to the present day, including the line of guitars DANIEL *saw in the old house. A huge photograph of a snow leopard dominates the room, its face staring down.*

DANIEL *stares at* RICHARD. *His eyes fill with tears. He fights them back.*

DANIEL: Don't know why I'm getting tearful . . . got no right to . . . I didn't even know him.

He looks up at ALICE.

DANIEL: Am I like him?

ALICE: I don't know yet . . . Maybe.

DANIEL: So what's behind all this weird cloak-and-dagger messages? Why wasn't he on the family tree?

ALICE: I have no idea.

DANIEL *stares at her.*

ALICE: I really have no idea . . .

DANIEL: What? That doesn't make sense . . . he must have been removed for a reason.

ALICE: It's totally inexplicable to me . . . I know Stephen wouldn't have left him off on purpose. Nor would anybody have asked for him to be removed. Why should anybody to that? As you see it was on an earlier copy – it's just an accident, a very bad mistake.

DANIEL: Yes – because it looks like he's been airbrushed out of the family.

ALICE: I know what it looks like . . . (*Carefully tidying the pictures.*) That's what I want you to tell Charles and Rebecca, the explanation is that it was simply a mistake, a horrible clerical error.

DANIEL: Why aren't you talking to each other? This is idiotic . . . ! Go and tell him yourself – Charles is just down the passage now . . . Or I'll go and fetch him –

ALICE (*sharp*): No, Daniel. Not just now.

Her tone stops DANIEL. *He looks at* ALICE.

DANIEL: I can't believe somebody like you . . . having to send these surreptitious messages –

The picture of RICHARD *stares at him.*

ALICE: As you know, in all families things happen. From the

outside they may not seem too impossible to solve, not too difficult to fix, but inside the family they have a huge significance, and if mishandled can cause real ruptures . . .

DANIEL: You mean I'd muck it up . . . if I tried to be more than a go-between?

ALICE: No. (*Simply.*) I just think it's best to do it my way, Daniel.

DANIEL (*staring at* CHARLES *and* REBECCA *when young*): And Charles and Rebecca – they've been keeping up a front for the whole of the reunion, but underneath . . .

He lifts the picture of RICHARD *in the leather coat right up to his face. He is clearly fascinated by it.*

DANIEL: Have you got any more pictures? Or is that it?

ALICE: I have one more . . . not as good as those . . .

ALICE takes one more photograph out of the drawer.
RICHARD is sitting in a squat position on the floor. He is in a long flowing shirt. He is barefoot. His hair is wet. He's staring out with a very piercing stare. His face looks grave and rather beautiful. Yet there's something unsettling about his stare.

DANIEL: He doesn't look so much like me there . . .

ALICE: Will you take the message to Rebecca? That it was a mistake – that it was just that. And ask her to reconsider my request?

ALICE stares at DANIEL.

ALICE: Please.

INT. ERNEST'S MANSION FLAT. BEDROOM. EVENING.
RAYMOND *wakes, in the late-evening light. For a moment he thinks he's alone, then suddenly he lets out a startled sound. In the corner of the room in the shadows is sitting the bulky shape of* PETER, *the moon-faced son of* ERNEST.

134

RAYMOND: Bloody hell! . . . Thought you were my wife for a moment!

PETER *stares back at him with his peaceful smile.*

RAYMOND: What are you doing here? (*Then realising this sounds ungrateful.*) It's good of you to stop by . . . It's just . . . I'm not at my absolute best . . .

PETER (*watching him for a moment*): Though I could visit you. You missed our appointment.

RAYMOND: Yes, I'm sorry . . . I got unwell. (*Ironic grin.*) As a few people at the banquet may have noticed! . . .

Pause. PETER *smiles.* RAYMOND *stares at him, wondering what he wants.*

PETER (*quietly*): I thought you made a wonderful speech.

RAYMOND: Really? Not sure that's the universal opinion . . . But thank you . . .

PETER (*suddenly beaming*): Hedgehog up my jumper! . . . I like that . . . I thought since I know my way round the kitchen here, I might cook you supper?

RAYMOND *surveys the ungainly looking* PETER, *who he now sees is clutching a rather grubby plastic bag.*

RAYMOND: Are you sure?

PETER: I am sure, yes.

RAYMOND: Well, why not! It's got to be better than the vegetable gruel . . .

INT. ERNEST'S MANSION FLAT. KITCHEN. EVENING.

PETER *is in the middle of cooking. A mountain of eggs are visible and a whole lot of ingredients – mushrooms, bacon, pepper, onions, prawns and one or two more exotic choices.*

PETER *is moving around the kitchen with great confidence, with the effortless movements of a dancer as if he is in his absolute element cooking. The evening sun has deepened into really dying light.* PETER *keeps on dodging to avoid bumping into the* NURSE, *who is standing in the kitchen being very watchful.*

NURSE: I *have* to be here . . .

PETER (*to* RAYMOND): So do you like the look of it so far? I hope you will say 'this is a truly great omelette'.

RAYMOND: Yes – I like eggs.

PETER: But it's gloomy, this place, isn't it?

(*As he cooks.*) I grew up in the big house, in Grosvenor Street . . . you could get lost in that house . . . and there was lots of light. But now they're selling *this* too – won't get to cook here very much more. (*Smiles*) My father doesn't let me cook for him as much as I'd like to anyway . . .

RAYMOND: Right . . . You look really at home here, Peter.

PETER *is moving fast as if preparing a meal in a rushed restaurant kitchen.*

RAYMOND: Been thinking about *my* father . . . Can't get this picture out of my head that Stephen found. Of my father dancing!

He was always so in control, my dad, serious and gruff – grouchy but in a powerful way. To see him do that! Dancing like a pixie . . .

He wanted all his workforce to call him by his Christian name, but behind his back people were terrified of him . . . I know I was! (*We see the melancholy in* RAYMOND*'s eyes.*) Sometimes I still wake up to him shouting at me . . .

(*Watching* PETER *cook.*) My mother wasn't terrified of him. He married a calm woman, still and peaceful . . . maybe I did the same.

At least I thought I had!

Forty-eight hours ago people thought I was dying – and now no sign of my wife . . . and no sign of my son!

(*He looks up at* PETER.) Don't know why I'm telling you this?!

PETER (*smiles his benign smile*): This is my own composition – this omelette. Midsummer night omelette.

INT. HOTEL ORGANISER'S OFFICE. EVENING.
The big lamps are on. Light falling outside. ESTHER *and* STEPHEN *are sitting staring intently at a website of family records.* ESTHER *is really gripped, concentrating hard.*

STEPHEN: I'm in the nineteenth century. The Dents who moved to Pennsylvania . . . and at the same time his brother came back from Jamaica. But now we need to go back a bit further . . . and goodness I must go soon, it's nearly dark . . .

ESTHER (*staring at the screen*): Yes and I must really get back to Raymond. Daniel is with him at the moment, but I ought to take over . . . (*Reluctantly she moves.*)

STEPHEN: Esther . . . I just want to ask you something . . . (ESTHER *turns*.) On your website (*he's waiting for her website to come up*) I do find it curious . . . you've got all these pictures of gardens . . . Is that of some special significance?

We see pictures on screen of a suburban garden, full of interesting pointed structures for climbing flowers. And then another picture of a garden with different-shaped structures, strange tall pots.

ESTHER: It's all the same garden actually. My garden. I kept experimenting with it . . . a few wild ideas. I put it there . . . it was just a hunch in case any of these Dents around the world . . . any of them shared the same passion. I know that doesn't mean we're related . . . and it's such a universal passion of course.

Was it a crazy thing to do?

STEPHEN: No, no . . . (*He smiles.*) Not particularly scientific,
but neither is it crazy . . .

*For a moment they both stare at the strange garden on the
screen.*

EXT. BLOCK OF CONVERTED FLATS. DUSK
DANIEL *stands pressing the entryphone outside an industrial
building that has been converted into luxury flats.*

REBECCA's voice: Yes?
DANIEL: Rebecca? . . . Hi, it's your messenger . . .

INT. STAIRCASE/FLAT. DUSK
DANIEL *walks up the very modern staircase, all concrete walls
and metal banisters.* REBECCA *is standing at the top calling
down.*

REBECCA: Keep coming up . . .
DANIEL (*calling up at her*): This isn't what I imagined I – (*As
he reaches her.*) Not where I thought you'd live at all.
REBECCA: Really? Hi . . .
She gives him a small kiss on the cheek.
DANIEL: It's a bit austere, isn't it?
REBECCA: Is it? . . . So you don't want to come in then?

INT. MODERN FLAT. DUSK.
We cut to DANIEL *moving into the big flat, a mixture of narrow,
snaking modern passages and a very large central sitting room.*

DANIEL: Blimey! – Doesn't anyone in this family live in a nice
138

normal cramped flat?

REBECCA: Yes. I do. (*Looking at him.*) This isn't my flat.

DANIEL: It isn't?

REBECCA: I'm flat-sitting for a friend, Sal, who's in Hong Kong for six months. (*She indicates, the décor on the walls and various surfaces.*) None of this is mine. All the decor, everything here is somebody else's.

DANIEL (*surveying the room*): None of this is yours? I don't believe there isn't something of yours here.

REBECCA: A few tiny things . . .

They're moving down the narrow passage into a very modern kitchen, the dusk is just hovering on the edge of night outside.

REBECCA: How did you get on? . . . Did you see Alice?

DANIEL: Oh yes . . .

REBECCA: And did you give her the message?

DANIEL: Yes.

REBECCA: And what did she say? How did she receive it? (*She turns.*) Tell me exactly.

DANIEL: I think she was saddened by it.

REBECCA: Right. (*Quiet, turning away, to herself.*) I don't forgive her . . .

DANIEL (*looking at her closely*): I also saw some pictures of Richard . . .

REBECCA *has her back to him.*

REBECCA: You did? . . . (*Pause.*) Wasn't he beautiful, my brother?

DANIEL: Yes. He was . . .

Alice wants you to know the reason he's not on the family tree is – there was simply a horrible clerical –

REBECCA (*interrupting him, suddenly erupting*): If she says it's a mistake, a simple MISTAKE, that is just not true! (*She yells.*) THAT IS NOT TRUE!

DANIEL (*startled by her passion*): Whatever happened . . . it can't be Alice's fault . . .

REBECCA: You think! You think that's so?!

Isn't it such an incredible thing? – the whole fucking event is staged – the whole fucking reunion, and there's no sign, no mention of my brother! He's only been dead for less than three years, for Chrissake! . . .

DANIEL (*softly*): Rebecca . . .

REBECCA: It's the most unbelievable inept, cruel stupid thing –

DANIEL: Sssh, Rebecca . . . sssh.

He catches hold of her trying to calm her.

REBECCA: All the time, the entire weekend I've had to play at being up . . . being breezy and a good guest, don't spoil the fucking party! Because I was dammed if I was going to be blamed for making a fuss about nothing and ruining everything. That way it would become all about me – *not Richard.* If I'd gone round haranguing everybody, they'd just say, 'Oh she's never got over it, poor girl!'

But it *wasn't* a mistake. And it's not NOTHING – it matters more than anything . . .

She is crying in his arms.

REBECCA: I can't bear it . . . I can't bear it, Daniel.

DANIEL *is holding her close. She nuzzles her head into his chest.*

REBECCA: Oh, Daniel . . .

She touches him as she cries, he starts to kiss her.

REBECCA: No, not that . . . please . . . Just hold me . . .

A pause as her crying gets less. DANIEL *is rubbing her tears softly off her cheek. He starts to kiss her again.* REBECCA *moves.*

REBECCA: That's not just holding me . . .

DANIEL: It's getting dark in here.

As the scene has unfolded in the kitchen, dusk has gone and

140

it is now almost dark.

REBECCA: Yes . . . (*she touches him for a moment, then she moves.*) There's a light here . . . somewhere (*She stumbles about in the dark.*) I've only been here for six weeks . . . I don't even know where the lights are?!

DANIEL *opens the fridge door, and the light spills from it giving the room a glow.*

REBECCA (*softly*): Clever thinking . . .

Pause. DANIEL *stands by the fridge staring at her.* REBECCA *meets his gaze for a moment and then turns away.*

REBECCA: I'll show you the rest of this spotless flat . . .

We cut to the main reception room. The lights flicking on. A very large and fairly empty room. DANIEL *whistles.*

DANIEL: Big room, Rebecca. (*He turns.*) Thirty-five by fifty-five . . .

REBECCA: Just like that . . . You can do it just like that? . . . Have you got your gizmo with you . . . ?

DANIEL: Oh yes, here is my 'gizmo' . . . (*He smiles.*) An EDM as us professionals call it –

He holds it up, points it straight at REBECCA.

DANIEL: And yes it's thirty-five . . . (*he moves up to her*) . . . by fifty-five . . . Exactly.

He starts to kiss her again.

REBECCA: I don't think this is a good idea, Daniel . . .

DANIEL: Why not?

REBECCA: Because I'm in a bit of an emotional . . . whatever you'd call it . . . (DANIEL *kissing her*) . . . in a highly strung state . . . (*She touches his lip.*) And *you've* been drinking . . . whisky by the taste of it. And we don't know each other . . .

DANIEL: Of course we know each other.

He kisses her.

DANIEL: We know what each other is thinking all the time . . . Right from the first moment we saw each other.

141

REBECCA: You don't know that, Daniel.

DANIEL: Yes I do.

REBECCA (*breaking away from him*): I'll show you what Sal
calls the gallery passage . . . her own little art gallery . . .

They go out into a thin bare passage.

DANIEL: Thirty-four by nine. Where are the pictures?

REBECCA: I took them down . . . they were really depressing.

He catches REBECCA *again, a very sexual kiss, their bodies
close up against the wall.*

REBECCA: Daniel . . . Please.

*She stops him for a moment, holding his head, touching his
forehead.*

REBECCA: Shouldn't you be being all aggrieved . . . that
would be better, wouldn't it? More normal . . . ? You
should be a bit outraged –

DANIEL: Why should I be that?

REBECCA: You know why.

DANIEL: Being asked to be a go-between, you mean . . . ?
The cousin from the suburbs humbly carrying messages
. . . nobody will tell him why . . . but they expect him to
keep on doing it?

REBECCA: Something like that.

DANIEL: And dressing him up in Richard's clothes in the old
house?

REBECCA: We didn't 'dress you up' . . . we thought you
would like that coat.

DANIEL: And you were right. So I'm not outraged, no . . .

He kisses her.

DANIEL: And you *knew* I wouldn't get like that. (*Stares
straight at her.*) Didn't you . . .

He kisses her, touches her hair. She stops him again.

REBECCA: You're not worried then? A dead brother . . . who
you look rather like . . . it doesn't bother you?

DANIEL: No . . .

142

REBECCA: Not worried at all?

DANIEL *staring at her, touching her.*

DANIEL: Not at the moment.

He kisses her.

DANIEL: It used to be very common I believe . . .

REBECCA: What?

DANIEL: Kissing cousins . . .

REBECCA: And I'm the older cousin . . . I ought to know better . . . I ought to put a stop to it.

They kiss, a very sexual kiss.

DANIEL: But you're not going to?

REBECCA: Gently . . . gently, Daniel . . .

We dissolve to an image of the little prince staring down at us through the banisters of the staircase in the old town house. We stay on his face for a moment as he stares directly into the camera.

Credits.

PERFECT STRANGERS

Part Three

OPENING CREDITS

We see the camera moving along the family tree. Then images of the young CHARLES, RICHARD *and* REBECCA *playing together, and the image of the young* VIOLET *and* EDITH *living wild in the woods. And then the photograph of* RAYMOND*'s dancing father slowly dissolving into the image of* DANIEL *as the little prince.*

INT. ERNEST'S MANSION FLAT. DINING ROOM. NIGHT.

The long dining-room table covered in beer and food and a huge omelette in the middle, in pride of place. It is already half eaten.

PETER *and* RAYMOND *are eating heartily and in silence. The Nurse opens the door of the dining room and lets in* ALICE.

RAYMOND: Bloody hell, this is good . . . I'm suddenly terribly popular.

ALICE: Raymond, I thought I'd just drop by to see how you are, I hope it's not too late . . . (*She smiles, staring at their feast.*) Well, I can see it's not too late.

RAYMOND: You embarrassingly find me knee-deep in more cooked eggs . . . Peter's made this most amazing omelette . . . it's an extraordinary concoction, full of everything you can ever put in an omelette. Sit down and have some . . .

ALICE: No, I couldn't, I've just eaten –

RAYMOND: I bet you'll succumb in a minute!

We were in fact just about to go next door, with more omelette on our laps and watch one of Ernest's collection of old British war movies . . .

You can help us choose.

INT. ERNEST'S MANSION FLAT. SITTING ROOM. NIGHT

We cut to the sitting room. PETER, ALICE *and* RAYMOND *are*

147

sitting facing us in front of the television. They all have plates of omelette on their laps. The fake electric fire is on, lapping its electric flames. The credit music of the old war film is just blaring out.

RAYMOND: Never seen this one, Peter –

PETER: This is good. You'll like this one.

RAYMOND: Jack Hawkins – as long as it's got Jack Hawkins.

We see the credits 'Jack Hawkins in Angels One Five'.

PETER: You see, it has. He plays the commander of the airbase whose nickname is Tiger – and the main pilot's name in the story is Septic . . . honestly, you'll see! It's quite exciting all the same . . .

RAYMOND: What could be better!

ALICE: Midsummer night – and it's so cold . . .

RAYMOND *glances at* ALICE *as a slight shiver goes through her. She is sitting close to the fire.* ALICE *sees him watching her.*

ALICE: Too many memories this weekend. It's like we're waiting for somebody else to get rid of them, isn't it? . . . Or at least ease them a bit.

RAYMOND: You mean Stephen? Stephen's going to straighten things out?! With the funny things he finds . . .

ALICE: I wasn't thinking of Stephen . . . (*We see deep sadness in* ALICE*'s eyes.*)

RAYMOND (*seeing this, with warmth*): Jack Hawkins isn't going to make you cry, is he? . . .

ALICE: No . . . Oh no (*She smiles.*) This will be good . . . watching the film here. I'm fine . . .

It's just sometimes looking at old photos can be terribly sad . . . can't it? . . .

The fake electric flames lapping.

RAYMOND: Yes . . .

He stares into the flames. He sees the picture of his father dancing.

RAYMOND: Not always . . . but yes . . .

The phone rings. RAYMOND *picks it up.*

RAYMOND: Esther! Where've you been?!

ESTHER'S VOICE: Oh, I've just been exploring something, finding out about something.

RAYMOND: I've been trying you, your phone was off.

ESTHER'S VOICE: I'm coming now. Isn't Daniel there?

RAYMOND: No, no, I've got loads of company, but our son isn't here.

ESTHER'S VOICE: Why ever not?

RAYMOND: I don't know – he came here . . . told me a great story – and then buggered off.

INT. MODERN FLAT BEDROOM. NIGHT.

REBECCA *and* DANIEL *lie naked in bed, but slightly apart.*
DANIEL *watches* REBECCA, *her manner distant.* DANIEL *glances at the time. It is ten to twelve.*

DANIEL: I oughtn't to spend the night here.

REBECCA (*quiet*): No, you oughtn't.

DANIEL: But I'm going to . . . (*He touches her.*) If I may . . . I should have called my father . . . That's where I should be . . .

REBECCA (*softly*): Yes, you ought.

DANIEL: It's been an amazing few days.

REBECCA (*quiet*): I'm glad to have been a *part* of your amazing experience.

DANIEL: No, you know what I mean . . . Stephen is right!

REBECCA: Stephen, *Stephen* is right?!

DANIEL: Yes, he said if you take any family and get them together and get to them to stay up long enough, the stores will come tumbling out. He said there were at least three great stories in any family and he's right too . . . it's

149

an addiction, a sort of legal narcotic . . .

REBECCA *quietly reaches for her mobile phone and starts dialling.*

DANIEL: Blimey – who are you calling?

REBECCA: Charles . . . I call him every day, sometimes twice a day . . . wherever he is in the world . . . in the middle of my working day . . . whatever I'm doing, I make sure I call him.

I'm not going to lose another brother . . .

EXT. NIGHT STREETS/INT. BEDROOM.

CHARLES *is sweeping along a broad empty street. He is wearing the long leather coat. We intercut with the bedroom.*

REBECCA: Charles, where are you?

CHARLES: Walking home . . . got about a mile to go . . .

REBECCA: Take a cab.

CHARLES: Why?! . . . What am I going to meet in the middle of Fulham? Some marauding lions . . . ? (*He swerves as he walks.*) Snakes coming out of the cracks in the pavement?! . . .

(*Softer.*) I'm all right, Becks . . . more than all right! . . . Now that I'm not in the hotel . . .

Every step I take, I put a little more distance between me and that gathering, between me and the family . . .

REBECCA (*softly*): Charles . . .

CHARLES *is walking purposefully but he's started to walk in the middle of the road, the night traffic having to swerve to avoid him.*

CHARLES: I'm taking healthy gulps of air . . . getting it all out of my system.

It's a great sky here, Becks! . . . You should take a look, take a look now . . . We don't stare at the sky enough in this city . . . (*staring up*.) It's a wonderful sky tonight, maybe I'll see something . . . an asteroid, a UFO, or a giant picture of Alice . . .

What do you think?

REBECCA: You're still drunk, aren't you, Charles? . . .
(*Softly*.) Stop somewhere for a moment . . .

CHARLES: I told you I'm walking it off!

But thank Christ that is over, Becks! . . . You must feel it to . . . We'll never do that again . . . Need never attend a family reunion ever, ever again . . .

REBECCA (*softly*.): Get home quickly, Charles . . .

REBECCA *rings off.* DANIEL *has been watching a very private communication between brother and sister.*

DANIEL: Is Charles OK?

REBECCA *pulls the covers around her. Her head deep in the pillow.*

REBECCA: Tonight he's OK . . .

She is staring at DANIEL.

REBECCA: Daniel . . .? (*Her tone is very quiet.*) You're thinking about Alice, aren't you?

DANIEL: Alice?

We see a shot of ALICE *in her suite, in her elegant evening clothes, ready to go out to the restaurant.*

DANIEL: I was a little. Yes. I love her . . . (*He smiles*.) I mean, I adore her . . . the sort of person you dream about . . . as a surrogate mother . . . the ideal alternative parent . . .

He turns towards REBECCA.

DANIEL: She is a very surprising, interesting woman.

REBECCA (*very quiet*): She is. In many ways.

DANIEL: I'm thinking, Rebecca . . . (*He touches her gently*.)
Maybe . . . you know, because I'm part of this family . . . but I'm looking in from the outside – maybe there are things . . . things I can do? Maybe there are connections I can make . . .

151

DANIEL *and* REBECCA*'s faces close.*

REBECCA (*softly, but intense*): I don't want you to
misunderstand, Daniel.

DANIEL: I don't misunderstand . . .

REBECCA: Are you sure . . .? Promise me one thing . . .

DANIEL: Yes?

REBECCA: Don't start thinking you can put the pieces back
together . . . Promise me . . . because you can't.

DANIEL *stares at her.*

DANIEL (*softly*): Of course I can't . . .

We stay on him for a moment.

We see early cine-film of the three children, CHARLES,
RICHARD *and* REBECCA, *together when they were very
young, and then a photo of* RICHARD *as an adult, staring
out with his startling piercing eyes. And this dissolves into
the picture of the little prince.*

*The sequence continues with a subjective shot of the
camera approaching a wall with the adult* REBECCA *and*
CHARLES *sitting on it, with a space in between them.
They're beckoning towards the camera for us to approach.
Then we see the subjective movement of the camera become*
DANIEL*'s approach as he joins them on the low wall, where
they are sitting sipping wine, as if at a party in the country,
people moving out of focus in the foreground.* DANIEL *is
filling the space between them on the wall. A close warm,
intimate atmosphere between the three of them.*

The sequence ends with DANIEL *opening his eyes.*

INT. MODERN FLAT. DAY.
He wakes in REBECCA*'s modern flat. We see his POV of*
REBECCA *who is standing at the foot of the bed, sipping a mug of
coffee. She is dressed ready for work.*

152

REBECCA: Time you were awake.

DANIEL: Is it very late?

REBECCA: No, it's seven thirty . . . I've got to go to work
soon. How are you feeling?

DANIEL: I'm fine . . . I was dreaming, a great dream . . .

REBECCA *moves into the kitchen.*

Time cut.

DANIEL *approaches, wearing jeans, his shirt open, just
beginning to button it.* REBECCA *is sitting at the end of the
white table pouring him some coffee.* DANIEL *surveys the
empty walls with the few bits of decor from the owner of the
flat.*

DANIEL: None of this is yours?

REBECCA: No, I told you, everything here belongs to a friend
of mine . . .

DANIEL *stares at her.*

DANIEL: I would love to know more about you, Rebecca . . .

REBECCA: I thought you said you knew what I was thinking
about all the time . . .

DANIEL (*looking straight at her*): You may have no pictures of
yourself anywhere here . . . but Alice showed me
pictures of you, photos of you, as a kid and because I
have a very good visual memory I can still see them . . .

REBECCA: Can you really? Which ones especially?

We see pictures of her growing up.

DANIEL: One I particularly liked was you half turned away
under a tree, in the shadows, with a big birdcage behind
you.

He watches her.

DANIEL: You're thinking . . . you wish last night hadn't
happened?

REBECCA: No, that's not what I'm thinking . . . (*More softly.*)
You got that one wrong . . . I just don't think it should
happen again. Not for a bit . . .

153

DANIEL *watches her for a second and then abruptly picks up the phone.*

REBECCA: What are you doing? Who are you calling?

INT. MANSION FLAT/MODERN FLAT. DAY.
We cut to the splendid old bathroom in the mansion flat.
RAYMOND *answers the phone on the wall, and he then sits on the lowered lavatory seat. He is in his striped pyjamas.*

RAYMOND: Daniel! At last he surfaces! . . . Where are you? Where've you been?

DANIEL: Oh, you know, I've been round and about . . . catching up on family business. (*He watches* REBECCA *out of the corner of his eye.*)

RAYMOND: Oh, for goodness sake, you can tell me where you've been.

DANIEL: Where are you?

RAYMOND: Where am I? You know where I am.

DANIEL: Are you up and about?

RAYMOND: I'm in the bloody loo! – I'm stuck here, practically under house arrest.
He indicates ESTHER *who is tapping at her laptop in the main sitting-room area.* RAYMOND *can see her through the open bathroom door.*

RAYMOND: Your mother is obsessively tapping away on her computer about something she won't talk to me about. And I'm told I can't stir from here for another week . . . When are you coming to see me?

DANIEL: I'll come to see you later on today . . . You sound like you're getting better all the time.

RAYMOND: You're dead right . . . so you've got to come and help negotiate my release.

DANIEL: Absolutely.

154

DANIEL *rings off and looks at* REBECCA.

DANIEL: You must be crazy if you think we're going to let go now.

REBECCA: What do you mean?

DANIEL (*lightly, effortlessly*): We come to this weekend . . . all these relations we haven't met . . . My dad sees this picture that intrigues him about his father . . . and I see a picture of when I was a tiny boy, dressed in an extraordinary way.

We're not going to shove off back to the suburbs before we've found out what was going on?!

REBECCA: What's all this about 'shoving off to the suburbs'? That's not like you, Daniel –

DANIEL: Besides, we're all going to go to the party in the country together . . . Irving is going to get me an invitation.

REBECCA: Well, I won't be there – because of course Alice will be going.

DANIEL: You can't let that stop you –

REBECCA: Oh yes I can . . . Martina was saying it would break her heart if Charles and I weren't there. (*She laughs slightly.*) But I'm still not going . . .

DANIEL (*watching her*): I need another message for Alice.

REBECCA: No, you don't.

DANIEL: Oh yes I do. She'll want to know what happened when you heard her message.

REBECCA: Don't you have to get to work?

DANIEL: All I've got today is a couple of houses in Isleworth . . . (*He smiles.*) They can wait . . .

REBECCA: I'm not sure you'll want to take any of the messages I might send her now.

DANIEL: Of course. I'll take any message.

REBECCA: For instance . . . (*her tone matter-of-fact*) Like . . . 'Tell the truth for once, you bitch.'

She stops and looks at him.

REBECCA: You see . . . I told you you wouldn't take it . . .

EXT. LARGE LONDON HOUSE. DAY.
DANIEL *approaches the big house in the leafy London square. A subjective shot pulling him towards it. He rings the bell. A sharp-featured elderly woman answers.*

MINTY: Who are you?

DANIEL: I'm Daniel . . . I've come to see Alice. Are you Minty? (*He hesitates.*) The housekeeper?

MINTY: How did you know that? I don't know who you are . . . But then nobody tells me anything . . . I suppose you better come in . . . what does it matter anyway? There's nothing left to steal here.

INT. ALICE'S FLAT. DAY.
DANIEL *enters the flat moving through the tidy sitting room with* MINTY *grumbling on in the background.*

MINTY: I'm not at all well today . . . it just gets worse and worse . . . my back . . . (*We hear the noise of builders.*) And there's this terrible racket from next door.
DANIEL *passes into the big old kitchen with lots of pots and pans hanging up.* ALICE *is on all fours, washing the kitchen floor.*

ALICE: There you are, Daniel . . . you always arrive sooner then I expect . . .
DANIEL *looks at the sight of her on all fours, doing something so menial as washing the floor.*

DAINEL: Can I help you do that?

ALICE (*standing up*): No, Daniel . . . You can't help me wash

156

my kitchen floor . . .

Time cut.

> DANIEL *and* ALICE *sit opposite each other at the big kitchen table.* DANIEL *has a mug of coffee in front of him,* ALICE *has a cup of tea.*

ALICE: Do you have a message for me, Daniel?

DANIEL: Maybe.

ALICE: What does maybe mean . . .?

DANIEL: Rebecca said, 'You should tell Daniel everything' . . .

We see she doesn't believe him.

ALICE: I'm sure she didn't say that, Daniel.

DANIEL *(staring straight at her)*: If you tell me, I can help . . . maybe, you know, resolve things . . .

ALICE: And how would you go about that?

DANIEL *(undeterred)*: Because like a really useful go-between I'm trusted by both sides . . . *(He looks at her.)* I think . . . and I've already pieced together a few things.

ALICE: You think you've pieced it together? . . .

DANIEL: Something happened to Richard, didn't it . . . ? I mean, before he died . . .

There were these three children who were very close – but whose parents were never around, the sort of people who just don't seem to know what to do with children, who shouldn't really be allowed to have children . . .

But these three siblings were terribly lucky because there was this other person available, who gave them love . . . and introduced them to all sorts of things, books, art . . . encouraged them . . . was chic and a little mysterious – everything you could want as you're growing up . . .

And this arrangement suited everybody perfectly, the semi-adoption of these siblings . . . and Richard was in many ways the glue that held it together – because he was the most outgoing, the most fun, the one in the middle who always had ideas . . .

And then something made Richard grow away . . . and *that* left very big scars . . . (*He looks up at* ALICE.) How did I do?

ALICE: That's quite close, Daniel . . . in some ways, not in others . . . (ALICE *stares at* DANIEL *for a moment.*) The children's parents . . . they were not cruelly neglectful – they were just totally bound up in their marriage . . . Louis, their father, had this marvellously undemanding job, it seemed . . . He worked for something called the Metal Box Company . . . it was the last moments of British business abroad being gin and tonics on the verandah, as the sun goes down . . .

We see a series of photographs of British businessmen abroad in Argentina – the social clubs, the polo games, the drinking, and the women in dark glasses. We see a picture of the siblings' parents among all of these.

We cut back to ALICE. DANIEL *is watching her closely.*

DANIEL: A wonderfully lazy way of doing business . . .

ALICE: Yes. (*She smiles.*) They are rather lazy people, Louis and Margaret, I will grant you that. And Margaret was quite determined to go wherever Louis went, they always managed to wrangle a posting where there was sun, sand and plenty of cheap alcohol.

We see a photograph of drunk British businessmen, leaning over a railing staring down on to an exotic beach.

ALICE: As soon as they were old enough the children were packed off to boarding school . . . And all the time there was this aunt by marriage living just down the road from the children . . . someone who was just a little younger than their mother . . .

We see a hazy live-action shot of ALICE, *turning towards the camera, on a sunny summer day, a romantic picture, as seen from a child's POV, a person with authority, but also mystery.*

ALICE: Someone who'd given up her job to live with her affluent husband in the country and have children. Only as hard as she tried – the babies didn't come . . .

We see her, in flashback, moving in the hazy summer light.

We cut back to ALICE *in the kitchen staring directly at* DANIEL.

ALICE: So we got very close, the children and me . . . It's not unusual –

DANIEL: No . . .

ALICE: – that children find themselves being brought up by an aunt or an elder sister.

She sips her tea.

ALICE: I remember the day Richard got into university –

We see in live action the siblings' parents standing together with drinks and RICHARD *laughing and leaning on* ALICE's *shoulder, as* REBECCA *and* CHARLES *watch them, also celebrating.*

ALICE (*VO*): Louis and Margaret were looking at me almost shyly . . . Like this is all *your* doing, well done indeed, thank you very much – it was like something entirely separate from them . . . And then almost immediately Louis was on the phone, talking about whether he was going to make it back to Buenos Aires in time for a polo match . . .

We see a live-action shot of RICHARD *and* ALICE *together, as* RICHARD *flourishes his acceptance letter, his ticket to university.*

We cut back to ALICE. DANIEL *meets her eye.*

DANIEL: And then whatever happened, started to happen . . . didn't it?

We see a shot of RICHARD *stretched out, lying on a sofa, a charming flirtatious smile. He is eating cherries. We cut back to* ALICE.

ALICE (*a momentary look of sorrow in her eyes*): The first

159

moment I noticed something was one day when Richard
was taking photographs . . .

EXT. LAWN. DAY/INTERCUT WITH KITCHEN.
We see RICHARD *taking pictures on a lawn. It is summer. He is
staring straight at us, the shot is subjective.*

RICHARD: Come on, you slackers . . . less wooden please!
  We only see RICHARD.
ALICE (*VO*): He's taking a photo . . . everything is normal
    . . . and suddenly he stops . . .
    RICHARD, *very nonchalantly, glances down for a second at
    the grass.*
RICHARD: What was that . . . ? Did you feel it? . . . I heard
    something going on down there. Some sort of noise . . .
    (*He smiles.*) A ripple of something going on there.
    RICHARD *pauses with the camera staring straight at us.*
ALICE (*VO*): It was like he was testing us – seeing if we would
    say 'We can hear it too' . . .
RICHARD: There . . . Did you feel it? It's probably nothing . . .
ALICE (*VO*): I felt at the time he knew we wouldn't agree
    we could hear anything, but it was like he had to
    mention it.
RICHARD (*nonchalant smile, becoming his charming self*): Must
    be some very busy moles, furiously burrowing together
    . . . partying down there. Come on now, let's try to get a
    decent picture! . . .
    We cut back to ALICE. *Her tone is calm and crisp.*
ALICE: Then a few months later we were going to the theatre.
    Even when the kids were adults, we regularly went out
    together . . .
      We were in the foyer of the theatre, picking up our
    tickets early, before going off for a meal, and there was a

woman there in the queue . . . one minute Richard was
talking perfectly normally . . .

INT. FOYER OF THEATRE. DAY/INTERCUT WITH
KITCHEN.
RICHARD *goes up to the woman in her fur coat. He makes tiny
little movements, jabbing movements, with his hand at her.*

RICHARD: You're wearing my brother.
The woman looks astonished.
The skin, the fur – his fur . . . You're wearing my
brother . . . Is that whimsical? Is that embarrassingly
emotive? No, I don't believe so, madam – because here I
see is one of his feet . . . (*He is fingering the fur around the
woman's neck.*) His toenails, just here, just by your cheek
. . . all through the evening his toenails will be brushing
you there . . . How does that feel . . . does it feel as soft
as it did before? . . . No, don't look over there, nobody's
going to help you, nobody's going to lift a finger . . .
*The woman is pressed up against the side of the box office.
Tense close-ups of* ALICE, REBECCA *and* CHARLES.
CHARLES *intervenes, pulling* RICHARD *away.*
We cut back to ALICE *in the kitchen.*
ALICE: We thought because it was the time a lot of animal
rights activity was just becoming fashionable – maybe
Richard was going through a very extreme phase . . . But
then he refused to stay at university . . .
DANIEL (*quiet*): After all the teaching you'd done . . . that
must have been hurtful –
ALICE: I didn't *teach* him. It wasn't like that . . . but of course
I watched him grow, he was very gifted.
Children turn their back on things they're good at all
the time – it's like a switch goes and that's it – and there

161

is *nothing* you can do about it . . . but this was a very stark example of that.

INT. PAWNBROKER'S SHOP. DAY/INTERCUT WITH KITCHEN.
RICHARD *is surrounded by a multitude of objects.*

ALICE: Because he went to work at a pawnbrokers, I don't suppose you thought they still existed, you know the three gold balls dangling there – I have to admit I never ever thought I'd set foot in one. But there he was, my Richard, behind the counter . . . We all went to see him at his invitation . . . He said he *had* to be there . . .
We see REBECCA, CHARLES *and* ALICE *moving in the shadowy shop, surrounded by all the objects, the guitars, strapped along the wall.*

ALICE: Because he needed to meet interesting people, weird people, it would help him in his chosen career, being a novelist . . . He said he was planning a huge work called *The Labyrinth* about secret passages and cities, what was under the pavements of a city . . .
RICHARD *beams in the shadows. He indicates certain objects.*

RICHARD: Touch that, go on, touch that . . .
What do you feel? . . . Can you feel it? It's warm, isn't it . . . and sort of tingling? . . . No, no, not those, the ones over there, feel them, touch them. Ssh . . . touch them carefully . . .

ALICE: We were standing there on that summer's day . . . it broke my heart – touching these various objects. Could we felt certain things going through them? Richard keenly watching us, waiting for our answer.
The image of them standing awkwardly touching the objects in silence.

162

ALICE: And of course in one way it was obvious he was ill, but suddenly it would all go and he would be back to normal.

RICHARD (*grins*): Kind of spooky in here, isn't . . . ?! Let's go out, let's go to the river.

ALICE: And I thought it would be all right. I read about how these things can be temporary. I got him to see various doctors and all the diagnoses were very different and inconclusive . . . because he could be so charming when he wanted.

We see him in the kitchen with ALICE, *sitting where* DANIEL *is now sitting, across the table.*

RICHARD: I know it's upsetting . . . I know you don't believe me . . . (*Touching her hand gently.*) Don't worry . . .
We cut back to ALICE.

ALICE: But then there was an unignorable incident. Very comic in a way, I suppose – involving a lot of buses.

DANIEL: A lot of buses . . . ?

ALICE: Yes . . .

EXT. STREET. DAY/INTERCUT WITH KITCHEN.
RICHARD *is turning towards the camera, moving down the street. Urging us on with a charming smile.*

RICHARD: Come on, we're going to get you on a bus, Alice – because I haven't seen you on a bus for years and years.
CHARLES, REBECCA *and* ALICE *move together towards* RICHARD *and the bus stop.*

ALICE: And he stood there, 'And I'll take care of this,' he said. And as each bus came, he'd stop it, because it was a request stop. He'd get on the bus to check it, he'd listen for a second and then refuse it, wouldn't let us get on wave the bus away.

163

A montage of buses drawing up. And then RICHARD
*climbing aboard by the conductor, listening for a second, then
getting out and waving the bus on.*

ALICE: Until he finally found one that he approved of and let
us get on.

RICHARD *urges them upstairs and supervises them sitting
down in a particular seat in the top of the bus.*

RICHARD: Do you feel it? . . . Can you feel it . . .? This is
really good . . .

We cut back to ALICE.

ALICE: You know how some buses vibrate very badly when
they are not moving – when they pull up at a stop, or at
the lights, and sort of shake . . .

DANIEL: Yes – it's when the engine revs are set too low, the
petrol isn't running through the engine fast enough, and
it's fighting to stay turning over –

ALICE: Oh, I wish you'd been there that day and been able to
say that! . . .

(*Smiles.*) Not a mechanic among us . . . of course it
wouldn't have made any difference really.

We cut back to the bus.

RICHARD (*to the others on the bus*): Why do you think it's
vibrating like that . . . ? Feel that . . . ? The incredible
echoes going through the whole bus and then out
beyond . . . if you concentrate on how much it's shaking,
it's really interesting, isn't it?

If you listen to the noises around one, *really* listen to
this bus, have you ever done that before? Listen to the
city and feel it, AS IT REALLY IS – And what is really
being said . . . What the noise is saying.

ALICE (*very quiet*): What is it saying, Richard . . . ?

RICHARD: It's saying many things – sometimes, like now, it's
saying . . . 'There's no other way', (*He bangs the side of
the bus.*) 'There Is No Other Way!' . . .

We cut back to ALICE.

ALICE: He became more and more unpredictable. He began drinking heavily . . . was always suddenly appearing . . . *She looks up. A subjective shot of* RICHARD *at the kitchen window.*

ALICE: Asking for money. He always wanted coins. . . and he walked everywhere . . . often he was barefoot. He walked across the whole city – because the noises that the buses and tube trains were making were too complicated he said. If he heard them he had to start talking back, so it was simpler to walk everywhere . . . But there were still moments he was wonderfully his old self.
We see RICHARD *carefully helping* ALICE *into her coat to go out, talking to her softly and lovingly.*

ALICE: And then somehow . . . (*There's deep sadness in her eyes.*)
MINTY *enters, she's standing in the doorway.*

MINTY: It's Richard, isn't it . . . you're talking about him?
MINTY *stands smoking, leaning against the wall in the kitchen, watching sympathetically. A sense of trust and familiarity between the two women.*

ALICE: And somehow it gradually became easier to make plans and not include him . . . Did I start that happening? (*Her voice falters.*) I'm not sure . . . I know that's what Rebecca believes, that I started it . . . And we did it surreptitiously because he still wanted to come, and he wasn't violent or anything, it just became more and more normal not to include him . . .

And then there was the picnic . . .
DANIEL: The picnic?
ALICE: A truly awful picnic . . .

165

EXT. HOUSE AND LAWN IN THE COUNTRY.
DAY./INTERCUT WITH KITCHEN.

ALICE: We were having Sunday lunch at my house in
 Buckinghamshire. My husband Robert had only been
 dead a couple of years . . . And I really loved to see
 Rebecca and Charles. And we were sitting having coffee
 after lunch . . . it was a perfect summer afternoon . . .
 and suddenly we looked up and there was Richard,
 coming across the lawn. I'll never forget it. He was
 carrying this rather nice picnic basket.
 We see RICHARD *coming from the far distance across the
 lawn, pleasant eager smile on his face, carrying a big picnic
 basket.* CHARLES, REBECCA *and* ALICE *watch him
 approach with foreboding.*

 ALICE *in VO and* RICHARD *both say the line at the same
 time.*
ALICE: And he says, 'We must have a picnic.'
REBECCA: We've eaten, Richard . . .
ALICE: And we say we can't . . . we've just had lunch . . . and
 he says, 'Oh, come on, I've found the perfect spot and
 I've bought the perfect picnic.'
 We see RICHARD *coaxing them across the lawn.*
ALICE: And so we follow him, first to the bottom of the
 garden . . . 'Isn't this the perfect spot?' he says.

 And just as we've all sat down, and he's started
 unpacking the basket he says, 'No, this isn't the spot.
 This spot isn't good enough.'
 We see images of this happening.

 And we get up . . . and he says, 'No, the perfect spot is
 just over here.' And we move over to the beginning of
 the wood, and we settle in the shade under a tree. And
 he says, 'This is much more like the perfect spot.' And
 then the same thing happens again. We've sat down, he

166

begins to unpack the picnic, and then he decides the spot isn't good enough, and then we're all off, and again and again this happens.

We see them moving through the wood with RICHARD *leading them, carrying the picnic basket.*

ALICE: And we get further into the wood, deeper and deeper. And then at last he says, 'This is it . . . this is the perfect spot'.' And we've ended up by some disgusting pipes, a drainage system.

And we just can't follow him down there by the pipes. I can't bear the idea of sitting there with him saying, 'Do you understand the significance of the noise these pipes are making?' None of us could cope sitting there that day and that happening.

And we lose him. We let him unpack the picnic, and we leave him there . . .

We see a shot of RICHARD *laying out the picnic glimpsed through the branches of the trees in the wood. His head down, giving them the opportunity to escape. And we see* ALICE, CHARLES *and* REBECCA *scurrying away.*

ALICE: We scramble away . . . we can hear him calling . . . He's completely surprised we've left him there . . . And then because we know he'll follow us straight back to the house . . .

We stay on RICHARD *looking for them in the wood, staring around and calling.*

ALICE: We get into the car and drive round and round in circles for hours, longing for him not to be there when we get back . . .

She is nearly in tears, but then the moment passes.

ALICE: He wasn't, in fact. He wasn't there when we got back. And it was not the only time we did something like that, not by any means . . .

And then one day he walked on to a railway line and

was hit by a train.

Silence.

MINTY (*smoking*): And that was the end of a beautiful boy.

DANIEL: He was ill . . . there was nothing you could have
    done.

ALICE: He was ill of course. Nobody gave him a definitive
    diagnosis. He wasn't schizophrenic. He didn't fit any one
    pattern.

She pauses for a moment as if stopping herself crying again.

ALICE: After his death . . . Charles got a posting abroad,
    Rebecca buried herself in her work.

DANIEL: And it was difficult to see them . . .

ALICE: There was a lot of pain for all of us obviously, guilt
    . . . Somehow every time I arranged to see them there
    was an excuse . . .

DANIEL: Until the idea of a great family reunion came up . . .
    You encouraged Ernest to hold it, didn't you – because
    it was probably something Charles and Rebecca had to
    attend? Among all those guests there were really only
    two you wanted to see –

ALICE: No. I don't agree with that, that's too simple. But of
    course I wanted us to have time together . . .

DANIEL: You *can* still see them.

ALICE: I don't know about that, Daniel.

DANIEL: I can help you. I really think I can. Let me . . .

The saucepans hung up around the kitchen begin to rattle.

MINTY: That bloody noise from next door.

DANIEL (*looking at* ALICE): Will you show me the house? I'd
    really like to see it . . . because I may have been here
    when I was small . . .

INT. ERNEST'S MANSION FLAT. DAY.

ESTHER *is tapping away on her laptop. She is surrounded by*

family histories of various 'Dents', printed out from the internet.
She looks up, RAYMOND *is watching her closely from the door.*

ESTHER: You're awake . . .

RAYMOND: Oh yes! . . . (*He stands at the doorway looking at
her.*) I've actually been watching you for about half an
hour.

ESTHER: Really?! (*She smiles.*) For half an hour . . . Why were
you doing that?

RAYMOND: I wish I knew what you were doing.

ESTHER: I'm just going back into my family . . . their history
. . . You've caught me at an exciting moment –

RAYMOND (*disbelief*): Exciting moment, really?

ESTHER: I'm just about to cross out of the nineteenth century
. . . dip into the eighteenth . . . following where the Dents
lead me.

RAYMOND: I see . . . You think that you're going to discover
something unexpected . . . romantic even?

ESTHER: I don't know . . . I've got a tiny sense about
something. Probably be disappointed –

RAYMOND: I ought to be beavering away too! – looking for
solutions to my father's picture . . . Remember him
dancing?! (*He glances around the shelves of books in*
ERNEST*'s sitting room.*) Probably the answer is right
here! . . .

ESTHER: You need to take things gently, you need –

RAYMOND: Don't say 'rest'. If I hear that word one more
time I'll have an instant relapse . . . (*He stares at her
sitting at her laptop, seeing how clearly fascinated she is in
her work.*) You're really wrapped up in it, aren't you?

ESTHER (*looking at the screen*): I've got to go back to work
tomorrow, I'm running out of time, so yes, I am pretty
wrapped . . .

INT. LARGE LONDON HOUSE. DAY.

The blinds are going up on the window of the main staircase.
DANIEL *moves up the stairs briskly, the light is pouring down.*
MINTY *is hitting the blinds so all the dust comes off them.*

DANIEL: Alice! There's this picture of me as a child – staring
down these stairs, dressed as a little prince . . . I don't
know what I was doing here – I have no idea at all . . .
(*He is staring down from the stairs at* ALICE.) But it was
just here, I think . . .
DANIEL *takes up the pose of the little prince.*
ALICE: I can't help you with that, Daniel, I don't remember
you standing there as a child.
DANIEL: I'm hoping that something really interesting lies
behind the picture. It's probably just a Christmas
party! . . .
DANIEL *moves off through the doors on the first floor.*
ALICE: Where are you going?
DANIEL: I just want to see the big cupboard again . . . have a
look inside.
ALICE *is following him.*
ALICE: You remember that from when you were little? Or
have you been here more recently, Daniel . . .?
DANIEL *stops, decides not to own up to his nocturnal visit.*
DANIEL: No, I must remember the cupboard, mustn't I, from
when I was little, this enormous cupboard . . .
*We cut to them moving through the big rooms on the first
floor. This time they are seen in daylight, with the blinds
open and the dust playing in the sunlight. We see all the
boxes, the damp stains, the rolled-up carpets. The old
heaters, the stained photos. The effect is a melancholic spread
of unloved family belongings.*
MINTY *is standing in the doorway of the big central room.*
MINTY: What a miserable sight, isn't it now, all this . . . Time

170

they burned the lot.

DANIEL *has reached the cupboard in the end room and starts looking through it,* ALICE *is watching him from the door.*

DANIEL *picks up a ruff, like from a fancy-dress costume.*

ALICE: Found something?

DANIEL: Possibly.

We see a grainy quick cut of the ruff around the neck of a small boy. In front of him the heads of other children bobbing around with fancy-dress headdresses on, little antlers and gnome hats. We see the hand of the boy going up to the ruff, pulling it away, as if it's uncomfortable, tickling his neck, and throwing the ruff to one side.

We cut back to DANIEL *in the present.*

DANIEL: Still can't remember really.

He stands up.

DANIEL: Thank you for letting me see that.

ALICE *smiles at his polite formality.*

ALICE: So, Daniel, what is your plan?

DANIEL: It's simple . . .

ALICE: Good –

DANIEL: You need to be all together again, Charles, Rebecca and yourself. There's an urgent need for that, isn't there? . . .

And you can use the go-between. I can be the instrument for that happening.

ALICE: And how would we manage that?

DANIEL: You send another message via me.

ALICE: I thought you didn't want to take any more messages.

DANIEL: The only difference is, this time the message needs to be a lie. (ALICE *watches him closely.*) Not much of one. A small lie, that's all it needs . . .

INT. HOTEL. POPPY'S OFFICE. DAY

The family tree is coming down, the boards are being removed.
STEPHEN *picks up bits of paper and puts them in boxes. In the middle of the room there is a table plan spread out on an expanse of white paper. All over it names have been crossed out, put in and rearranged.*

POPPY *is packing up. She is in a terrible state.*

POPPY: I've made so many mistakes, Stephen . . . ! I should
    have insisted we kept this office on all week . . . The last
    thing we need is to move now . . . because chaos is
    developing –
    She looks up and sees DANIEL *standing in the doorway of
    the office.*

POPPY: Chaos, Daniel!

DANIEL: In what way?

POPPY (*staring frantically at her table plan*): The party in the
    country of course! . . . It was to have been a *small* party
    because Ernest's wife Nazik's relatives are coming to
    celebrate from the Lebanon – to celebrate Martina's
    engagement . . . And they were to be joined by a select
    few from the reunion, people that were *close* – that's why
    the events were scheduled so near each other – it was a
    very good plan – but now all sorts of people want to
    come! It's ballooning into something it wasn't meant to
    be and nobody seems to want to say *no.*

STEPHEN: I was going to do something elaborate for each
    person, but now I've had to abandon it because the guest
    list keeps growing –

DANIEL: That's exactly why I'm here, to wangle an invitation.
    Irving was going to get me an invitation –

POPPY: Irving definitely will NOT be invited. If we're going
    to get as far as inviting Irving, we will be inviting
    absolutely everyone! We'll be up to the numbers at the

172

banquet . . . it's ludicrous – (*She stares despairingly at the paper with all the names scrawled over it.*) I can't even do a proper table plan yet. And after the disaster last time, I'm determined this one will be *perfect*!

DANIEL (*smiles*): You will let me have an invitation, won't you? Alice wants me to be there . . .

POPPY: Well, that might just get you in . . . (*She moves over to get an invitation card.*) Mind you get here on time, everyone must leave at least four hours for the drive, the traffic can be absolutely horrendous on a Saturday –

INT. HOTEL PASSAGE/FOREIGN OFFICE PASSAGE AND CONFERENCE ROOM. DAY.
DANIEL *is on his mobile phone in the passage just outside* POPPY'*s office. We cut to* CHARLES *answering his call while striding along a Foreign Office corridor, with an entourage of about three civil servants.*

DANIEL: Charles?

CHARLES: Daniel, hi, I'm just going into a meeting . . . What is it . . . ?

CHARLES *stops in the doorway of the conference room. We can see twenty people sitting around a long table, waiting for him to chair a meeting.*

DANIEL: Are you coming to the party in the country? I want to make sure you're coming because I'm going to be there.

CHARLES: Daniel, I've got all these people waiting . . .

DANIEL (*softly*): And I've got a message from Alice – she's not going to be there, Alice will definitely not be coming. I've just left her . . . and she gave me this message: 'Tell them under *no circumstances* will Alice be there.'

CHARLES (*very surprised by this conversation*): Right –

DANIEL (*his voice softly persuasive*): So you will come? It'll be great, all three together . . . I've been talking a lot about Richard to Alice and Rebecca –

CHARLES: You have? . . . I didn't know you knew about Richard . . .

People are watching CHARLES *from around the table.*

CHARLES: I'll call you.

CHARLES *goes into the meeting, sits at the table, shuffles his papers. His confident mood has changed dramatically, he seems deeply preoccupied.*

CHARLES: So, now, we're going to look at the . . . minutes of the Antwerp meeting . . . and especially at the contents of paragraph 809 . . . (*He pauses glancing at this phone seemingly losing his train of thought.*) 809 is on page . . .

CIVIL SERVANT: Page seventy-five.

CHARLES (*slowly*): Seventy . . . five . . . (*He stops completely, everybody looking at him round the table.*) Sorry, I'm suddenly feeling an incredible call of nature . . . it's absolutely shouting at me . . . So, if you'll excuse me . . .

INT. GENTLEMEN'S LAVATORY INTERCUT WITH MONITORING OF FOREIGN BROADCASTS BUILDING. DAY.

We cut to CHARLES *in a gentlemen's lavatory. A large old-fashioned space with heavy lamps. He is in a corner of the white-tiled toilets on his mobile phone. We intercut with* REBECCA *at the monitoring unit for foreign broadcasts. She is sitting in front of series of monitors supervising a couple of people who are closely watching the screens.*

In the distance in the lavatories a cleaner is washing basins.

CHARLES (*His manner is very flustered and emotional*): Becks . . .

174

REBECCA: Hi, how are you doing? I'm sitting here watching a Ukrainian broadcast, a Ukrainian cookery programme . . .

CHARLES: Daniel's just rung . . . he want us to go to the party in the country, and Alice is not going to be there –

REBECCA: Who says?

CHARLES: Alice says – via Daniel. She sent a very clear message . . .

REBECCA: I'll talk to Daniel –

CHARLES: Daniel also mentioned he knew about Richard.

REBECCA: Yes, he found out about it –

CHARLES: For some reason, Daniel knowing . . . suddenly made it . . . it was incredible what went through me . . . made it all seem like it had just happened . . . made it all fresh again. I'm in the middle of chairing this meeting, and I felt myself . . . (*He begins to cry.*) And I just began to feel in the meeting like I was going to burst into tears (*He is trying to fight the tears very hard.*) It's like a panic attack or something. I don't know why this should be happening just because Daniel phones me. I've go twenty people sitting round a table in there waiting for me . . . !

REBECCA: Let them wait . . . it's all right . . .

CHARLES: And there's a gentleman here who's cleaning the basins who's trying very hard to pretend he can't see a man crying on the phone . . . a man weeping in the corner.

He turns right in the corner, trying to be as private as possible.

CHARLES: Becks, it's just sometimes it seems so bad . . .

REBECCA: I know . . . it's OK. Just cry, why not? (*She's sitting there in front of the televisions.*) I get like that . . .

I involved Daniel. I sent a message via him, that there was *no way* we wanted to meet Alice to go over things. I told her that under no circumstances would we do that.

175

It seems to have worked.

CHARLES: Yes.

We hear the sound of heavy rain beginning, running down the big windows of the lavatory.

CHARLES: If somebody came in from the meeting to use the loos now, nobody here would ever think of me in the same way again. They're so used to seeing me in control – (*He glances across at the cleaner.*) I don't think I've cried in a lavatory before . . .

INT. CONFERENCE ROOM. DAY.

CHARLES *enters the room, people look up.* CHARLES *blows his nose, pulling himself together with remarkable agility.*
He sits, seemingly his normal stylish self, at the head of the table.

CHARLES: So . . . we can resume . . . back to Antwerp.

He glances up, the rain is falling heavily in the courtyard just outside the window.

INT. ERNEST'S MANSION FLAT/HILLINGDON HOUSE. EVENING.

RAYMOND *in the sitting room watching the same old British war movie. Jack Hawkins is talking over the radio to a pilot, calling out for Septic. The* NIGHT NURSE *is also watching with him. The sound of rain, really heavy, outside. The phone rings. It is* ESTHER. *We intercut with her at home in Hillingdon working at the computer. It is nearly dusk. Through the small French windows we can see the suburban garden with its tall decorative pots and unusual features being drenched in the rain.* ESTHER's *tone is warm, excited.*

ESTHER: Raymond how are you, my love?

RAYMOND: That's a nice greeting . . . (*He grins.*) You find me slumped in front of another of Ernest's old British war movies . . .

ESTHER: Daniel's just rung. He's got an invitation for this party in the country, Martina's engagement party . . . he seems all excited about it . . .

RAYMOND: Blimey, what's he up to? . . . He's definitely plotting away at something. Maybe he thinks he can unearth an inheritance, something that'll change his life –

ESTHER: He just wants to find out more about the family –

RAYMOND (*unconvinced*): You reckon? . . . Maybe *we* should go to this party? . . .

ESTHER: No, you know you can't. (*Her tone is intimate, excited.*) So are you missing me, my love?

RAYMOND: Of course! What is this? (*He grins.*) What happened to bring all this on?! (*He laughs.*) Have you been drinking?

ESTHER: No, no, not exactly! (*Excited smile.*) I've made a discovery and I wanted to tell you at once, because it is . . . well, it's not huge . . . but it's –

RAYMOND (*smiling at her enthusiasm*): Not huge?

ESTHER: But it is . . . I think it's lovely . . .

RAYMOND: Sounds good –

ESTHER: I pursued the Dents . . . I followed and followed my family, dug and dug . . . And suddenly I've hit this amazing relation that I'm descended from . . . I've found I'm directly *descended* from him . . .

We hear some Mozart playing in the background, an aria from The Marriage of Figaro, *'Non Piu Andrai'.*

The screen of ESTHER's *computer is changing all the time, the family tree with the Dents in the eighteenth century, and then we begin to see images of their property.*

ESTHER: Hear the music?

RAYMOND: What music?

ESTHER: I'll turn it up – can you hear it now?

RAYMOND: It's Mozart . . . You're not going to tell me you're descended from Mozart?! You're Mozart's great-great –

ESTHER: No, not quite. (*Her voice is softly excited.*) William Beckford.

RAYMOND: Who's he? Never heard of him . . .

ESTHER: William Beckford was an astonishing man. An aristocrat, a dilettante, bisexual –

RAYMOND (*grins*): That sounds good too –

ESTHER: He was taught by Mozart when they were both children, the eight-year-old Mozart had given him lessons in London, in Soho Square. They became lifelong friends . . . and my relation, William, claims to have written this music with Mozart . . .!

RAYMOND: Obviously he's a liar too!

ESTHER: Maybe – but the fantastic thing . . . the thing that gave me a really strange feeling, is – he put up these huge follies – these great garden follies . . . he just kept on doing it, couldn't stop!

We see the images on the computer screen. The huge towers and follies Beckford built. The incredible surrealistic tower of Fonthill Abbey. So thin and so tall.

ESTHER: He built this great ludicrous abbey, Fonthill Abbey, with an amazing tower that was so tall it fell down.

We see ESTHER staring from the images of the computer out through her French windows into her garden.

ESTHER: And who do you know who loves towers?! . . . I'm staring at the garden, Raymond, now, and there are my little abbey towers all over the garden, getting a bit soaked at the moment! Isn't it amazing!?

RAYMOND: That is good, yes. Don't start building any more until I get home, will you . . .

ESTHER: I really feel that there must be something in all this,

178

things in your family resurfacing after generations, swimming around in the gene pool – coming out in unexpected ways, unexpected places . . . (*she grins*) like Hillingdon . . .

RAYMOND: Yeah . . . that is quite exciting . . . (*He smiles.*) How about the bisexual part then? . . .

ESTHER *laughs. The* NURSE's *eyes flash, she's been watching the whole conversation.*

RAYMOND: I quite like the music your ancestor wrote! . . . I wish I could get into this discovery malarkey myself . . . might sort a few things out . . . I need to get rid of my jailers and into action!

We hear the Mozart louder and louder.

ESTHER (*softly*): Soon, you'll be well enough soon . . .

INT. MODERN FLAT. NIGHT.

The rain pouring down, sounding very loud through the modern flat. REBECCA *and* DANIEL *are snuggled up in bed together.*

REBECCA: God – it's a deluge. It hasn't stopped for three days! If it's like this tomorrow . . .

DANIEL: We'll be swimming round the party –

REBECCA: It'll be a disaster, if it doesn't stop . . . (*Looking straight at him.*) You promise she isn't coming?

DANIEL: I promise. The message couldn't have been clearer, could it?

REBECCA: Yes. Alice wouldn't lie about that.

DANIEL: She wants you to have a good time –

REBECCA (*watching him closely*): Why are you looking so excited about it?

DANIEL (*innocently*): Was I? . . . Because I'll be with you . . .

REBECCA (*Smiles, touching him.*) I was going to stop this, wasn't I? It wasn't meant to happen again –

179

DANIEL (*touching her gently*): But it has –

REBECCA (*touching his face*): When I first saw you in the hotel passage –

DANIEL: You thought Jesus, who's *this*?! –

REBECCA (*gently touching him*): Something like that . . . A stranger . . . but he's also my cousin –

DANIEL: And now?

REBECCA: And now? – I don't know (*softly*) Part lover . . . part replacement brother –

DANIEL (*firm but soft*): Not replacement brother . . .

REBECCA: No . . . (*kissing him*) You're right, not that (*looking at him*)

REBECCA: I don't know what you're hoping for tomorrow . . . It's only a big house Ernest's family once owned which is now a conference centre and golf course – it couldn't be less evocative of the family really . . . I don't know why Ernest's holding it there, it's like he's saying goodbye to his childhood memories –

DANIEL: That makes sense. (*He kisses her shoulder.*) I can't wait . . .

REBECCA: You aren't lying to me, Daniel?

DANIEL: Why would I do that?

REBECCA: You haven't disobeyed me . . . about trying to put the pieces together again?

The sound of the insistent rain.

DANIEL (*softly*): I wouldn't dare do that . . .

EXT. GROUNDS OF THE LARGE COUNTRY HOUSE. DAY.
The sound of the rain stops abruptly. Glistening wet grass in the morning sun. The camera tilts up to discover POPPY*'s sensible shoes, squelching in the mud. And then in wide shot we see* POPPY *is standing alone on a big expanse of lawn, the large country house behind her. She is staring across at the marquee. Between*

180

her and the marquee there is a muddy morass. For a moment her face is frozen in shock.

POPPY: Oh my God! . . . this is even worse than I imagined . . .
   The BOY ASSISTANT *is running towards her, sloshing through the mud.*
BOY ASSISTANT: The good news is – (*As he nears her, he just stops himself falling head first into the mud.*) The really good news is – No more rain! It's official!
POPPY (*Pulling herself together.*): Angus – it's going to be our greatest challenge . . . to bring this off . . . We'll need notices, notices galore. . . boards . . . we need to create walkways and paths . . . and we need boots, hundreds of boots . . .

INT. ERNEST'S MANSION FLAT. DAY
RAYMOND *wakes in the gloomy bedroom of the mansion flat, to be greeted by* IRVING *and* SIDNEY *standing and watching him.*

RAYMOND: Blimey, every time I wake up, there is somebody new at the end of my bed . . .
SIDNEY: Good morning, Raymond.
IRVING: Have you got some spare rope?
RAYMOND: Spare rope? . . . (*he stares back at them.*) No, I think I'm right out of that as it happens.
IRVING: We thought we'd tie up the nurse . . . (*Then he smiles.*) We're going to get you out of here, Raymond –
SIDNEY: Everybody else is going to this party, we thought why the hell should we miss out?!
RAYMOND: Absolutely, my feelings entirely. They won't let us in, will they – ?
IRVING: Ah! We have a secret weapon . . .
   Time cut.

181

We see PETER *turning in the sitting room as* IRVING,
SIDNEY *and* RAYMOND *join him.* RAYMOND *is in his
dressing gown.* PETER *is shuffling among the papers in the
large desk.*

PETER (*as he sees* RAYMOND): You want to come to my
father's party?

RAYMOND: You bet . . .

PETER: No problem. (*Turning back to the open desk.*) I'm just
poking about here, in his desk, because somewhere . . . is
his least favourite picture of me . . he keeps it right down
here.

PETER *produces a picture of himself working at the news-
stand on the concourse of Paddington Station. The
photograph captures him at the precise moment he is selling
an evening paper to a customer. That customer is* ERNEST.

PETER: Paddington Station, I worked there for eight years . . .
One day my father bought a paper from me by accident
. . . he had no idea I worked there . . . Martina took the
picture – she bought him along specially . . . Look at his
face!

ERNEST *looking startled and angry.*

RAYMOND: My father looked like that every time he caught
me watching television!

EXT. DANIEL'S CAR. DAY.
DANIEL *is driving* REBECCA. *Both are dressed for the party,*
DANIEL *is in a dinner jacket.*

DANIEL: This music OK?

REBECCA (*nods, her mood deeply preoccupied*): I've got a bad
feeling about this –

DANIEL (*softly*): Don't . . . It's going to be good. It's just a
party . . .

182

REBECCA *presses her face to the window.*

An image of RICHARD, *as an adult, roller skating along a corridor, looking back at* REBECCA *as he goes, his charming smile, the camera tracking behind him.*

We cut back to REBECCA's *eyes, deeply thoughtful.*

Then we cut to REBECCA *watching screens of foreign broadcasting.* RICHARD *is sitting next to her.*

RICHARD: Becky, all these different voices, amazing what you see, the different languages you understand . . . But you're not even near hearing what's actually going on . . . (*His voice is soft and affectionate.*) You may know all about flower arranging in Turkey, but to grasp what's really worth knowing (*his charming smile*), you need to turn to me . . . What I could tell you, Becky . . . if only you'd listen . . .

We cut back to REBECCA, *very close on her eyes.*

Then an image of ALICE *standing by a window, looking relaxed and full of joy, a pencil flicking backwards and forwards in her hand, as she is moving by the window, talking.*

We see three young faces, CHARLES, RICHARD *and* REBECCA *as children, watching her, truly rapt.*

We see RICHARD *walking barefoot along a London Street, his long leather coat scraping the ground, his arms waving. He seems very detached from the world.*

We then cut to REBECCA *and* RICHARD *sitting on a park bench.* RICHARD *is touching the rich lining of her coat – the same coat we saw* REBECCA *touching the first time* DANIEL *met her in the hotel room. Then* REBECCA *turns towards* RICHARD *and speaks to him in an imploring tone.*

REBECCA: Come back to me . . .

RICHARD (*stares back, his face calm*): Becky, don't start that. I haven't gone anywhere.

EXT. ERNEST'S CAR. DAY.
ERNEST *and* ALICE *ride in the back of his chauffeur-driven car.*
ERNEST*'s unimpressive vague manner, he is sitting dwarfed by
his own car. He glances out of the window.*

ERNEST: It seems set fair at last . . .
ALICE (*her manner contained, tense*): Yes . . . I believe so.

EXT. LONDON STREET. DAY.
IRVING, PETER, RAYMOND *and* SIDNEY *clambering into*
IRVING*'s very battered old Mercedes.*

IRVING: Apologies for the motor, I'm getting rid of it at the
end of the week . . . any boxes you don't like on the back
seat, just chuck 'em out –
SIDNEY: Wait till you see the house, Raymond, you'll be
gritting your teeth at the idea of Ernest growing up there.
(*Then remembering* PETER *is there.*) No offence meant.
PETER *just smiles.*
RAYMOND: I can just about remember the house . . .
IRVING *is busy chucking out the contents of the car, boxes
stuffed with papers.*
IRVING (*chucking the contents of the car out on to the pavement*):
Don't need most of this. (*To* PETER.) Just give it the
heave-ho!
RAYMOND (*settling down in the back*): Right . . . anybody got a
phone? I'm calling Esther when we're halfway there . . .
she shouldn't miss out on this either . . .
IRVING: Everybody in? (*He starts the engine and stares back at
his fleshy passengers.*) Very male gathering, isn't it?! OK,
hold on tight – We're going to make it in record time!

EXT. DRIVE AND GROUNDS OF THE LARGE COUNTRY
HOUSE. AFTERNOON.

DANIEL *and* REBECCA *drive down the long, straight and rather
bleak drive of the big house. They can see golfers standing like
sentries on the golf course, either side of the road, or squelching
their way through the mud, trying to see if it is fit to play.*

REBECCA (*looking out of the window*): You see, as I said – it's
nothing like it was when the family was here . . .
DANIEL *is driving looking determined, quietly excited.*
REBECCA (*staring across the grounds*): Imagine how big it
seemed when we were little and came to visit . . .
Then through the windscreen we see a series of POPPY*'s
notices painted on card and stuck to posts. Arrows and the
word 'Party' in incongruous red paint. Also 'Drive Slow!!'*
   *The house appears with a marquee in front of it. and we
see through the windscreen a cluster of guests, already there,
sitting outside the house or wandering in distracted circles.*
REBECCA: Everybody's arrived early – because of Poppy's
fierce instructions, 'Be late and you'll get no food!'
The BOY ASSISTANT *is standing ahead, directing the traffic.
He calls out to them. He is dressed in a dinner jacket, as
indeed are all the men.*
BOY ASSISTANT: Be very careful where you park . . . stay
strictly in the designated area. Otherwise your vehicle
will sink . . .
As they park, they see MARTINA *is greeting the crowd that is
milling in front of the house.*
MARTINA: Everyone's a little early, the marquee is just being
prepared now . . . it'll be fantastic inside when it's
finished! . . . Please make use of the gardens while you're
waiting –
POPPY *appears from within the marquee and calls out to the
crowd.*

POPPY: Keep strictly to the path . . . follow the arrows . . . don't venture off the path whatever you do! . . .

As DANIEL *and* REBECCA *get out of the car, they see* CHARLES *sitting in the shadows under a big cedar tree in the distance, watching everybody. They approach him.*

DANIEL: Charles, you beat us here . . .

CHARLES (*smiles, his manner relaxed*): Of course – I have my own special route.

DANIEL is looking over his shoulder, studying who is present among the guests and who is yet to turn up.

CHARLES (*following his gaze*): They look like refugees, don't they – at their own party?! It's funny, they couldn't book the inside of the house because there's a conference going on, so they're locked out of Ernest's old family home . . .

REBECCA: Come on, we can follow Poppy's arrows though!

We cut to them going down the long shadowy paths. The grounds have a series of secretive wooded paths that fan off from the formal garden.

REBECCA and CHARLES are moving ahead, DANIEL watching them closely as he follows.

REBECCA (*turning, calling back to* DANIEL): Got to keep to the path, Daniel – got to follow the arrows! . . .

We cut to shots of the guests packing their way along the boards on the grass, negotiating their way very gingerly in their evening dress, across the mud of the garden.

We see VIOLET, EDITH *and* GRACE *all dressed up for the party moving away from the formal garden into the woods.* EDITH *slips in the mud and falls to the ground.* VIOLET *smiles, stretching out a hand to help her, as* GRACE *stands in the shadows watching. The two sisters are back in a wood.*

We cut to another part of the grounds, a hill, overlooking the estate. The four fleshy men, RAYMOND, IRVING, SIDNEY *and* PETER, *appear over the brow of the hill,*

*walking straight towards us. They have left the mud-
spattered Mercedes parked on the grass. The house is nestling
below them, looking splendid.*

SIDNEY: There's the pile that Ernest grew up in . . . and all
because his father made a bob or two in the margarine
business! They only got rid of all this about fifteen years
ago . . .

IRVING (*to* RAYMOND): You wouldn't say no to a piece of
that, would you?!

SIDNEY: Sure beats putting up road humps.

PETER *stares down at the estate with a peaceful smile.*

RAYMOND: Yes . . . I know what I want to see first! Excuse
me . . . Got to check something out at once . . . See you
at the feast.

We cut to RAYMOND *moving down one of the shrouded
wooded paths, sloshing through the mud.*

RAYMOND (*muttering*): It's this way . . . (*He stops.*) Is it this
way? . . .

*He turns. He is standing where four dark shadowy paths
meet. He swings round, trying to remember, trying to pick
the right path.*

RAYMOND: It's this one . . .

*He comes out into a clearing. And there are the stone griffins
and the balustrade. The garden of the stone beasts from the
photograph. It looks very tidy and clean.*

RAYMOND: Jesus! It's all cleaned up . . . Got shiny faces . . .
the beasts . . .

RAYMOND *stands in the middle of the garden and moves
like his dancing father. The anarchic dancing pixie. A group
of guests are standing above the garden, staring down at
him.*

RAYMOND (*calling up at them*): Just imitating my father! . . .

The guests move on. RAYMOND *is alone in the garden, the
sound of the wind, the beasts looking back at him.*

187

We cut to REBECCA, CHARLES *and* DANIEL *moving along the secluded path towards where it emerges into the light.* REBECCA *and* CHARLES *are ahead of* DANIEL. DANIEL *watching them closely.*

DANIEL*'s mobile phone rings, and he drops further behind* REBECCA *and* CHARLES *to answer it.* REBECCA *laughs.*

REBECCA: Turn it off, Daniel! Shouldn't be taking calls here . . .

We see, from their POV, DANIEL *muttering hurriedly into the phone. He rings off and looks up.*

DANIEL: Just business . . . an enraged house buyer . . .

We cut to them coming out of the wooded area where three paths meet. One goes up the hill to a summer house, the arrow points along a path that leads back to the main house.

DANIEL: Let's go this way . . .

He starts off up the hill, towards the summer house.

REBECCA (*laughing*): That's off Poppy's route! . . . That's forbidden!

But they follow DANIEL. *He turns and looks back at them, urging them on.*

DANIEL: Come on, we're nearly there.

They catch him up.

From the hill they can see the golfers spread across the course, and the guests picking their way gingerly along the boards in the formal garden. The women teetering on their high-heeled shoes, a lot of them already muddied despite their best efforts.

The three of them stare at the view.

DANIEL: Remember this from when you were little?

REBECCA (*staring across the grounds*): Yes . . . it seems really right the golfers have taken it all over because even when we were kids it was like Ernest and his family were just temporarily in possession of the house . . . like they weren't meant to be here . . .

188

CHARLES: Playing at being landowners . . .

> DANIEL *sets off up the hill, aiming for the summer house.*
>
> *There is a quick cut of* RICHARD *forging ahead up the same path, turning and calling to* REBECCA *and* CHARLES.

RICHARD: Come on, you slackers, you are so out of condition!

> *We cut back to* DANIEL *standing in front of the summer house calling to* CHARLES *and* REBECCA.

DANIEL: This way, come on . . .

> REBECCA *and* CHARLES *follow* DANIEL *into the summer house.*

INT. SUMMER HOUSE. AFTERNOON.

Inside is the cool marble interior of the eighteenth-century summer house.

> *There is some rather rusty old garden furniture spread around. And a table set for tea, with a china tea service and a plate of biscuits.*
>
> *Sitting on one of the metal chairs is* ALICE.
>
> REBECCA *stops just inside the door as soon as she sees* ALICE.

REBECCA: That's brilliant, isn't it! –

> *She turns to* DANIEL. *Her tone really icy.*

REBECCA: You stupid little shit, I told you not to do this – I TOLD YOU. (*Her tone savage.*) But of course you thought you knew better, didn't you! You fucking idiot . . .

> ˙CHARLES *seems much less openly hostile to being in* ALICE'S *presence.*

CHARLES: Becks, ssh . . . Becks . . .

REBECCA : This is the single worst thing you could have done, Daniel –

DANIEL (*unfazed by her fury*): If people aren't talking . . .

189

REBECCA: Don't you dare start justifying yourself –

ALICE: Rebecca, please, don't blame Daniel, please . . . Blame me . . .

I'll go straight back to London, if you like, or you can walk out of here now and go back –

REBECCA (*lashing out*): I don't need your permission to go back to London, thank you . . . the last thing I need is your fucking permission.

Three little children suddenly run into the summer house. Two girls and a boy of about seven. They are dressed in elaborate party clothes, which are already a bit muddy.

GIRL: Oh, we can't hide in here, people in here! (*She looks at the adults.*)

ALICE (*smiles at the children*): I'm afraid this place is taken.

GIRL (*stares about her, trying to think of another hiding place*): Yes . . .

REBECCA: I'll take you back to the marquee, if you like . . .

GIRL: Oh no . . . we've got to hide! And we've got to be quick! . . .

The children run out of the summer house as quickly as they came in and start hurtling back down the hill. As they run they pass the old sisters, VIOLET, EDITH and GRACE, slowing climbing up the hill path.

For a moment REBECCA watches the children shoot off, disappearing away into the trees.

CHARLES sits by ALICE, leans forward. His manner is nervous, but he is determined to make something of the situation.

CHARLES: I'm going to pour myself some tea . . . since it's been thoughtfully provided. Does anybody else want to join me?

ALICE: No, but I can do that –

CHARLES: No, it's fine. I'll do the tea.

The china rattling, the noise almost surreally loud in the marble summer house.

ALICE: It'll be a bit cold . . .

CHARLES: It is a little, but drinkable, I think . . .

During this exchange DANIEL *has been watching the three old sisters slowly but purposefully climbing the hill path.*

DANIEL (*suddenly*): I know you think what I have done is underhand . . .

REBECCA *has her back to him.*

DANIEL: And probably misguided –

REBECCA *doesn't move.*

DANIEL: But there's just one thing I want to say and then I'll leave you alone.

And the one thing is – and I don't want this to seem presumptuous, but I'm both part of the family and yet I didn't know any of you a few days ago . . . and that gives me, I think it gives me, a unique sort of point of view, and what I want to say about Richard is this . . . (*his tone forceful.*) I know there's all this guilt about excluding him . . .

A shot of the sisters climbing and climbing the hill path, their determined walk.

DANIEL: But you couldn't have done anything . . . there's this pattern in the family, *a pattern that recurs.* If you know anything about the story of Violet and Edith, how they lived in the woods during the war, how they removed themselves from their parents and their sister, how they've been in a different world ever since really, *it's in the family* – don't you see! . . . And it came out again in Richard. This force pulling him away, and once it had reappeared, it was bound to happen – him growing away from you and everybody, there was nothing you could have done . . . nobody could have stopped it . . .

We see the two little girls, the young VIOLET *and the young* EDITH, *walking and walking down the long straight wartime road, and then* RICHARD *walking barefoot on the streets of London, his long leather coat brushing the ground. The sound of tea being poured brings us back to the present.* CHARLES *has filled all the cups. Once again the china rattles alarmingly in the stillness in the summer house.*

DANIEL *looks at them. He has put his case passionately.*

DANIEL: I just wanted to do something . . . I wanted . . . however unlikely it may seem, I wish I could make a difference . . .

He moves to the door. The old ladies have reached the top of the hill, and have passed the summer house. DANIEL *watches them recede along the path for a moment.*

REBECCA: Daniel, don't go.

DANIEL *turns.* REBECCA *has sat by the tea. She is sitting very straight very still.*

DANIEL: Are you sure?

REBECCA: I am sure. I want you to hear this. Absolutely. Since this is your solution – your fantasy solution – to intervene, bring us together, and let the guilt melt away. Let it all slip off.

(*Quietly.*) So I think you should see the results of your efforts, Daniel.

(*She is staring straight at* ALICE.) Every day, every single day, I think about what we did to Richard . . .

ALICE (*very quiet*): I'm sure we all do.

REBECCA (*very sharp*): *Please!* (*Looking at* ALICE.) Please . . . And I assure you I don't blame you as much as I do myself. (*Her tone very measured, but very cold.*) But, Alice . . . I don't forgive you. I don't forgive myself, and I certainly don't forgive you. We helped cause Richard's death . . . We shut him out . . .

(*She leans forward.*) And there's absolutely nothing else I want to say to you . . . ever . . . Do you understand, Alice?

CHARLES: Becks . . . No, it's best not –

REBECCA (*with complete finality*): Don't try to stop this, Charles . . .

There won't be a need for me to say it again, because I'm finding being with you, Alice, impossible, just like you found the mess Richard brought to your life unbearable, that is how I feel about you . . . Why, even now you can't bear to see his name put on the family tree –

ALICE: That is NOT what happened. It was a mistake –

REBECCA (*suddenly loud*): And what a perfect mistake it was, Alice! What a fucking stroke of genius. What a brilliantly *revealing* mistake!

ALICE *stares back, pale, impassive.*

REBECCA: So, Alice . . . I find thinking about you, talking about you . . . (*with real force*) how shall I put this? – very difficult, do you understand what I'm saying?

I'm saying I want no further dealings with you, ever. I don't want your calls, I don't want your letters, I don't want your messages, I don't want to hear your voice. It's so simple, Alice. I wish we'd never met you. It really is that simple.

ALICE *stares at her unflinching.*

CHARLES: Becks . . . !

REBECCA: We wanted a more glamorous mother, and we got one . . . and we paid the price. (*She spits the words out.*) And Richard did . . . most of all . . . My *brother* paid the biggest price . . . my beautiful brother . . .

She puts her face very close to ALICE.

REBECCA: Do you finally understand? Have you got it at last. (*She moves.*) Don't you ever try to contact me again.

She turns as she leaves the summer house.

REBECCA: Nice one, Daniel . . .

She has gone.

193

DANIEL *follows her out of the summer house.*

DANIEL: Rebecca . . .

She stops.

REBECCA: Don't you dare start explaining . . . (*she looks at him for a moment*): You promised you wouldn't do this . . .

REBECCA *begins to move off, then she stops and turns, stares at* DANIEL *directly, her tone incredulous*

REBECCA: You think talking about patterns helps?

Her voice cracking, there are tears in her eyes.

REBECCA: You think that HELPS! . . .

Her tone is forceful and passionate. DANIEL *cannot answer her. She moves off.*

DANIEL *pale and shocked, turns watching* ALICE *through the window of the summer house.* ALICE *is sitting impassively.* CHARLES *is leaning towards her gently, touching her arm, talking to her softly.* DANIEL *re-enters the summer house.*

CHARLES: Alice . . . she was taken by surprise . . . it was the shock of suddenly finding us all together . . .

ALICE (*quiet*): No, no, it wasn't. I know that's what she feels . . .

CHARLES: It won't last.

ALICE: Maybe it won't . . . (*Her voice quiet.*) And possibly it will. Now if you could just both leave please.

DANIEL: Is there . . . Is there anything I can get you?

ALICE: No. I would really appreciate you both just leaving me here for a moment. In a little while I have to make my speech at the party, in the marquee, welcoming everyone. It was my turn to do it . . . and I just need to go over it in my head –

CHARLES *and* DANIEL *hesitate about leaving her alone in the summer house.*

ALICE: Please, I'm fine . . . just go.

They look back at ALICE *sitting very calm, very straight.*

EXT. HILL PATH. LATE AFTERNOON.
We cut to DANIEL *and* CHARLES *standing side by side on the hill, staring over the grounds.* DANIEL *is looking very shocked, very upset.* CHARLES*'s manner is quiet, contained. The sun is just beginning to go down behind them.*

INT. SUMMER HOUSE. LATE AFTERNOON.
We cut back to ALICE *alone in the summer house. She is crying, real sobs of grief, wracking her body. She gets up, trying to regain control, but the sobs take over her whole body. She stands curled away from us in a corner, weeping.*

EXT. HILL PATH. LATE AFTERNOON.
We cut back to DANIEL *and* CHARLES.

DANIEL: I'm sorry . . . that was very foolish.
CHARLES: No . . .
DANIEL: Yes, it was a ludicrous idea that I could make a
    difference –
CHARLES: As you said, if people aren't talking then
    somebody's got to make them –
DANIEL: It *was* a fantasy, my plan – Rebecca was right. And
    I've made things worse . . .
    *They are both staring out across the formal gardens,
    watching the guests moving on the now muddy boards across
    the grass.*
CHARLES: Every day I see him . . .
DANIEL: Richard?
CHARLES: Yes . . . it doesn't matter where I am . . . last year I
    walked into a little supermarket in Mexico and saw his
    face, suddenly by the counter, it was incredible . . .
    He stares down.

195

CHARLES: But at least something came out just now . . .

DANIEL: No forgiveness.

CHARLES: From Rebecca, no.

It was the fault of all of us of course . . . I never blamed Alice so much – but maybe I didn't love her quite as much as the other two did either . . .

He is watching an unremarkable-looking plump elderly man moving carefully in the formal garden below.

CHARLES: My father . . . see down there . . . bumbling along . . . no doubt thinking about his next holiday. His whole life he seems to have been on a permanent holiday . . .

The camera pans along the path to find the SIBLINGS' MOTHER, *some distance away in the formal garden.*

CHARLES: And there is my mother . . .

CHARLES *watches her for a moment. One of the children has kicked a ball down the hill and it has landed at the feet of the* SIBLINGS' MOTHER *in the formal garden. The children are urging her to throw it back to them, and she is dithering, not knowing whether to step off the boards and into the mud to reach the ball. She makes a half-hearted movement, trying to reach it while remaining firmly on the path.*

CHARLES (*as his mother does this*): How unfair things are . . . there is my mother – who happily neglected us all . . . almost literally handed us over to Alice . . . And yet we feel nothing, no hate – nothing.

DANIEL (*watching* SIBLINGS' MOTHER): Well, everybody at some time wants alternative parents – glorious, exciting and only ever around when *you* want them to be –

CHARLES: Yes, but the difference with us – we did *get* an alternative mother. (*He watches his mother from the hill.*) There is something terrible about the way things have turned out, Alice wanting children so much, not having children of her own, and then she gets children, and she brings us up – and she is brilliant at it – (*He looks at*

196

DANIEL.) And she *was* brilliant at it, Daniel.

And then one child becomes an embarrassment, and so is slowly and deliberately excluded – until he dies. (CHARLES *has tears in his eyes.*) That's a sad story . . . as I said, a terrible thing . . .

DANIEL *touches* CHARLES'*s arm to comfort him, a little uncertain how much* CHARLES *wants physical contact. They stand, side by side, in silence.*

EXT. LAKE. EVENING.

IRVING *is squelching along in the mud on his own. A woman is sitting by the lake with her back to him. The light is just beginning to fall, rich summer evening light. The figure looks romantic and mysterious.*

As he reaches her, she turns, and IRVING *is surprised to see it is* ESTHER.

IRVING: Hello . . . I didn't recognise you at all. I thought who is this lovely apparition?! . . . You look wonderful!

ESTHER *is dressed very stylishly for the party.*

ESTHER: Thank you . . . I got a message from my husband saying, 'You must come to the party at once.' Of course he shouldn't be here – he's escaped from his sickbed! (*She is looking out across the lake.*) And I haven't been able to find him yet.

IRVING: I must own up, I was one of those who sprang him from his house arrest –

ESTHER: Right! . . . I'll withhold punishment for the moment. (*As she stares across the water.*) It's an amazing place this, isn't it . . .

IRVING: Yes . . . it *is* amazing. (*staring across lake*) But I would never want to live here . . .

ESTHER (*surprised*): Really?

197

IRVING: No, I will always be orbiting, Esther. That's what
I've realised now – I am a natural orbiter. (*He smiles.*)
And I intend to check out every corner of the globe. (*He
stares at the water, more serious. For a moment we see the
real* IRVING.)

    If I keep moving I know who I am . . . nobody else
may know – but I do . . .
We hear a church bell ringing from the distance.
    *We cut to the mouth of the marquee. We can see its lavish
decoration behind* POPPY. *The sound of the bell is much
louder. It is the bell of the chapel of the house. It is tolling
powerfully.*

POPPY (*yelling*): Dinner, everybody . . . time for dinner . . .
DINNER IS SERVED! . . . (*She turns to* ERNEST.) I let
them go all over the gardens and I hadn't thought how to
get them back! (*Anxious.*) Does it sound like a funeral?
(*The bell tolls on, summoning people to the meal.*)
ERNEST *is staring at the big house. The lights are just
coming on inside.*

ERNEST: How foolish it is, isn't it, Poppy, to have sold all
these houses . . . and just be living in hotels . . . and
rented apartments . . .

    Why don't I know where I want to live at the end of
my life . . . ?
POPPY *is spreading out the table plan in front of him, on the
first table inside the marquee.*

POPPY: Please, Ernest, concentrate . . . look at the table plan
. . . Is it all right? I've worked and reworked it . . . and I
have no idea if I've got it right now.

ERNEST (*not bothering to look*): I'm sure it'll be perfect,
Poppy . . .
*We cut to one of the broad paths leading towards the
marquee. The chapel bell is tolling insistently.*
    DANIEL *is walking by himself, still shocked and upset. He*

sees REBECCA *is walking a little further ahead on the same path. He quickens his pace to try to reach her.*

Suddenly SIDNEY *is by his side.*

SIDNEY (*waves his hand towards the house, at its glowing windows*): Money . . . all this money! . . . Imagine what it'd be like living here . . . . This was Ernest's home! . . . If things had been a little different, we could have had a share, you and I.

DANIEL: Maybe . . .

SIDNEY: Come on, Daniel – don't pretend you're not interested! You and me are about the only people here who are not too snobbish to say we'd love a bit more money! . . . Even Irving is more interested in the travel . . . It's you and me!

DANIEL *catches* REBECCA *up. She walks purposefully in the shadows, not looking at him.*

DANIEL: Rebecca . . . (*He implores her to look at him.*) Rebecca . . .

DANIEL *is moving alongside her, trying to engage with her. She totally ignores him, quickens her step to get away from him* DANIEL *stops on the path, watching the people moving ahead of him in the shadows. We cut back to* REBECCA. *As she moves we see she is sobbing. We cut back to* DANIEL.

DANIEL: Sidney, you go ahead, I'm not going into the meal just yet . . .

DANIEL *stands, still watching the guests disappear. He is shocked and upset.*

DANIEL: I should never have come . . .

Suddenly he hears his name being called. Somewhere RAYMOND *is calling him.*

RAYMOND'*s Voice*: Daniel . . . Daniel . . .

DANIEL *swings round on the path, trying to make out where it's coming from. The little girl who ran into the summer house is standing in the shadows.*

GIRL: Somebody's calling you.

DANIEL: Yes, I can hear . . . (*He looks at the* GIRL.) How did you know it was for me?

GIRL: Because you looked lost . . .

DANIEL: I'm trying to make out where he is . . .

The GIRL *points down one of the dark shadowy wooded paths.*

GIRL: I think it's that way . . .

DANIEL *sets off down the dark wooded path. Behind him he can hear the bell ringing out calling people to the meal. In front of him, somewhere through the trees, is his father. He is getting closer to his voice.*

RAYMOND'S VOICE: Come on . . . where the hell are you!? DANIEL!

DANIEL *comes out at the end of the path. He finds himself at the back of the house. His father is standing there, beckoning excitedly.*

RAYMOND: There you are at last! Come on! You've got to see this . . . in here . . . You've got to see something we've found –

DANIEL: We'll miss the meal! We've all been called . . .

RAYMOND: Bugger the meal. Come on!

INT. LARGE COUNTRY HOUSE. EVENING.

RAYMOND *and* DANIEL *enter the house, going through a side entrance, and down a passage.* RAYMOND *seems genuinely excited,* DANIEL *intrigued to see his father so animated.*

RAYMOND: Come on, quickly, it's this way.

STEPHEN *is standing in a doorway ahead of them. To get to him they have to cross the hall.*

RAYMOND: It is Stephen who found it . . .

They reach him.

200

STEPHEN: Well, I found it, but Raymond interpreted it . . .
it's just –

*A woman wearing a conference badge spots them and calls
out sharply.*

OFFICIOUS WOMAN: Excuse me! Who are you?

RAYMOND: Who are we, Madam? Good question.

OFFICIOUS WOMAN: Only conference guests are allowed in
the house, can't you read the notices? Party guests are
allowed to use the basement toilets and that's all . . . Do
you want the basement toilets?

RAYMOND: No, we'll pass on the basement toilets. (*They
move on.*) It's all right. Our family owned this house!

OFFICIOUS WOMAN (*calling after them*): And don't put mud
everywhere! . . .

*They walk through the hall and into a smaller room now
being used by the conference centre as an office. It is stuffed
full of filing cabinets and clumsy office furniture. But behind
the filing cabinets a mural is visible, an Edwardian copy of a
seventeenth-century painting decorating the inside of an
alcove. Staring straight out from the mural, his gaze meeting
DANIEL's immediately he sees it, is the little prince, standing
proudly in exactly the same costume, complete with the
unusual decorated shoes and the big ruff, as DANIEL is
wearing in the photograph. The little prince in the mural is
in exactly the same pose as well.*

DANIEL: There it is . . . There is the little prince . . . There I
am!

RAYMOND: Great, isn't it!

STEPHEN (*authoritatively*): It's an early twentieth-century
copy of a Venetian mural . . . I think . . .

*We see DANIEL staring at the eyes of the little prince. And then
we see the grainy images of the childhood party in the
London mansion, the ruff coming away and the children
spread out in front of DANIEL in their pirate and goblin and*

201

Robin Hood costumes.

DANIEL: I remember the party – just . . . and I found the ruff
(*he touches the mural*) in the London house the other day,
and I found the shoe . . .

*We see all the children staring at him in their costumes in the
grainy flashback.*

DANIEL: I must have been the only one not in a normal pirate
costume!

DANIEL *turns to* STEPHEN *and* RAYMOND.

DANIEL: But what does it mean? . . . Why was I dressed after
the picture? What was this room used for? . . .

RAYMOND: Aha.

STEPHEN: It was used as a study when Ernest was growing
up here –

DANIEL: So? Just as a study . . . What does that tell us?

RAYMOND: I think it might tell us quite a lot. (*He grins.*) But
you're *not* heir to his fortune! Come on now, outside
again!

DANIEL: Where are we going now?

RAYMOND: You won't regret it, worth missing the salmon
mousse for.

EXT. GARDEN AND PATHS. EVENING.
*We cut to them going down the broad wooded path, the one that
leads into the garden of the stone beasts. We see the photograph of
the little prince staring after them. They enter the garden of the
stone beasts. We see* RAYMOND *turning in the garden, in the
middle of the lawn, swinging round like his father did.*

DANIEL: So this is where your father's picture was taken!?
This was where your father was dancing!

DANIEL *runs up the steps and looks down from the stone
balustrade, like* RAYMOND *as a child did in the photograph.*

RAYMOND (*calling up to him*): I was standing there, yes, watching him . . . and of course what I've realised – what Stephen has helped me realise – what I've remembered for the first time . . . was what was really going on in that picture! . . .

We see the picture of DANIEL*'s* GRANDFATHER *dancing and the dark trees behind him.*

RAYMOND (*calls up to* DANIEL): Who do you see? . . . Look at the trees . . .

DANIEL *stares at the dark trees, moving in the wind. Simultaneously we see the camera moving in on the dark trees in the photograph.*

DANIEL: You mean someone else was there?! In the photograph.

RAYMOND: Exactly . . . somebody else was there . . , there was somebody else in the picture . . . you can just about make out an arm in the trees . . . Stephen has shown me.

We go in on the picture, trying to make out the figure.

RAYMOND: My father was dancing for the *other person in the garden* . . . The only person who made him feel joyful.

We see the photograph, we go deep into the shadows, we can just make out an arm and a shoulder.

And then the photograph moves, giving us a fuller image, as if it's revealing a memory, and there is HENRIETTA, *the alluring* HENRIETTA *that we saw in the slides through the stereoscope. The woman* DANIEL *was looking at in the veil. And then we see her in an ornate bedroom in a Venetian hotel. And then in live action, we see her standing in the shadows for a moment, in a momentary flashback, like a flick of memory.*

RAYMOND: Henrietta . . . Ernest's mother . . . the wife of my father's much, much elder brother . . .

STEPHEN: I always suspected from little bits of evidence I came across in the archive, they were having the most passionate affair . . .

We see, in a series of photographs, the eyes of RAYMOND's
father, as he dances, full of joy, and then the face of
HENRIETTA *watching him. And then the photographs melt*
into live action as we see HENRIETTA *watching, from her*
secret place in the trees, RAYMOND's *father and his*
extraordinary dance. He is dancing for her.

RAYMOND: It's terrific, isn't it?! My serious obsessive hard-
working father . . . and the only person that brought out
the joy in him – She was here, in the trees, and I was
watching! As a boy . . . the whole thing . . . but I didn't
realise!

DANIEL *stares across at the stone beasts, imagining*
HENRIETTA *in the garden. Suddenly he turns.*

DANIEL: And it wasn't? . . . (*Excited.*) I mean, I wasn't
dressed like the prince because –

RAYMOND: Yes! . . . It was for her too! Don't you see?

We see the grainy image of the party and the tiny DANIEL
standing there in his little prince costume. He looks up in the
flashback, there is the great shadow of his GRANDFATHER
looking down at him.

RAYMOND: We couldn't remember taking you to the party –
because we didn't . . . Your grandfather took you – And
he probably lied to us! – told us he was taking you to the
pictures . . .

He took you there because he knew *she* would be
there.

We see the images of the party, the GRANDFATHER *and the*
little DANIEL, *dressed as the little prince, entering. All the*
children, milling up and down the marble staircase.

RAYMOND: He must have hired the costume . . . no doubt it
was a form of signal . . . a sign of his continuing love for
her . . . a message –

We see a fine-looking woman, the elderly HENRIETTA,

looking excited and surprised as she sees the little DANIEL *as the little prince.*

Then we see little DANIEL *standing in the posture of the little prince in the mural on the staircase as the elderly* HENRIETTA *stands in the shadows with his* GRANDFATHER. *The* GRANDFATHER *calling out instructions, showing the boy exactly what posture he should take on the stairs.*

RAYMOND: You were a visual gift.

STEPHEN: The study where the mural is was Henrietta's study. They probably frequently met there . . .

DANIEL: To make love –

RAYMOND: No doubt to make passionate love! . . . You were a love token, Daniel . . .

In a grainy flashback we see the elderly HENRIETTA *staring at him, just touching his head. We see the elderly Henrietta watching the little* DANIEL *closely as he moves around the party. She beckons towards him and touches the buttons on his tunic, looking at the little dagger around his waist. The* GRANDFATHER *and the elderly* HENRIETTA *exchange looks at the party and then their hands reach out and touch each other as the little* DANIEL *stands between them, eating jelly. We see the little* DANIEL *pulling at his ruff as it's itching round his neck. The elderly* HENRIETTA *says very firmly to him, 'No, don't do that . . . we like you like that, Daniel'. The little* DANIEL *stops fiddling with his ruff but he's determined to get it off.*

Then we see the other children playing roughly as pirates, and the little DANIEL *taking off his ridiculous shoes and jumping in there too.*

DANIEL: My shoes came off . . . and I managed to get my ruff off too –

And in flashback the small DANIEL *is picked up in strong arms.*

DANIEL: And he took me away without my shoes – maybe
they'd had a quarrel and he wanted to leave . . . and he
couldn't be bothered to find them . . .

The little DANIEL *in the flashback turns his head to look
back as he's carried out. The elderly* HENRIETTA *stares back
at him out of the shadows of the hall. A receding shot of her.*

We cut back to RAYMOND. *He is standing among the
stone beasts. And then we see the picture of his dancing father
melting into the photograph of the little prince.*

RAYMOND: It's great. I love it! The two pictures, our two
pictures, are for the SAME REASON, Daniel.

We see HENRIETTA *in her veil staring out.*

RAYMOND: My father's secret life . . .

Time cut.

RAYMOND, DANIEL *and* STEPHEN *are moving down the
broad avenue. Ahead of them, in the distance, the marquee is
all lit up.*

DANIEL (*walking by his father*): Why does that make you so
happy, finding that?

RAYMOND: Because my father was such a severe old stick. All
my life he set me such high standards.

We see an image of his Father and HENRIETTA, *when
young, partially undressed, passionately kissing in front of
the mural.*

RAYMOND: To find he was so full of passion – it was
adulterous, he betrayed my mother – but it makes him a
lot more easy to cope with, I can tell you! (*He laughs.*) I
can start judging *him* for a change!

STEPHEN: I'll look discreetly – without offending Ernest – but
we must see what other evidence we can find, to back
this story up –

RAYMOND: You bet we will.

DANIEL (*quietly*): Well, it, makes *me* feel quite strange really

206

. . . I was a go-between even then – even when I was six!

RAYMOND: Who have you been acting as a go-between for, Daniel?

DANIEL: Oh . . . (*He smiles.*) Just family business.

RAYMOND: Don't worry too much about it – about being made to run errands – we are the Hillingdon contingent, after all!

They have reached a splendid view of the marquee, elaborately lit all the way round, like a spaceship.

STEPHEN: Poppy's special lighting . . . it looks good, doesn't it!

Standing outside the marquee, in the glow of the lights, is ESTHER. *A romantic image of her turning in her evening gown.*

RAYMOND: Esther . . . You made it! And you look fantastic . . . (*He embraces her.*)

ESTHER: Well, you shouldn't be here . . .

RAYMOND: Nor should you! Neither of us were invited.

ESTHER (*kissing him.*): But I'm glad we're here . . . You look very well suddenly . . .

RAYMOND (*putting his arm round her*): Just wait till you hear what I've got to tell you! (*Calling over his shoulder to* DANIEL.) Your mother has made a discovery too!

DANIEL (*watching them both, his parents excited and close*): Right!

RAYMOND: Your mother discovered that one of her relations wrote most of the works of Mozart!

ESTHER (*laughing*): Don't exaggerate . . . don't mock! Come on, or we'll miss the food.

DANIEL *watches them go towards the marquee together. He is standing next to* STEPHEN.

DANIEL: They're like your star pupils, Stephen . . . (*He watches his parents arm in arm.*) They really feel they've discovered something meaningful . . . Never seen my

207

mum look so young really – not for years.

STEPHEN: Good. (*His voice sombre.*) Makes up a little bit for
    my terrible mistake . . . on the family tree . . .

DANIEL: Leaving Richard off?

STEPHEN (*very quiet*): Yes. It's very upsetting. I've been
    thinking why it happened . . . I knew I had to check with
    Alice and the others about how to put Richard on the
    tree – just the bald dates or something else . . . and
    somehow that led to me leaving him off altogether . . . an
    awful thing to do to Richard . . . I don't know how I
    could have been so unprofessional . . . I'll never
    understand that . . .

*We see a very wide shot of the marquee glowing out in the
middle of the grounds surrounded by POPPY's special
lighting.*

INT. MARQUEE. EVENING.

*We cut inside the marquee, a high shot of all the characters sitting
around a very long L-shaped table, abiding by POPPY's seating
plan.*

*We cut to DANIEL. He is surprised to find himself sitting next
to SIDNEY and GRACE. He gazes around the table. IRVING is
pouring a drink for everybody.*

IRVING: Don't be afraid to guzzle, everybody – we have
    permission to guzzle.

    ESTHER *and* RAYMOND *are being very animated together,
    sitting next to* PETER. *We see* ALICE *is right at the opposite
    end of the table from the siblings.*

SIDNEY (*as if reading* DANIEL's *thoughts*): You were
    wondering how the hell did you end up with me?

DANIEL: Well . . . I was wondering how Poppy had done the
    seating plan . . . What she'd based it on? Especially as

she had so little warning who was turning up . . .

SIDNEY: There is a strange wisdom to it, isn't there?

DANIEL: Yes . . . (*He is very surprised.*) That *is* just what I was
thinking . . . (*He stares at the grouping of the characters.*)
Peter next to my father . . . Stephen near my mother . . .
the siblings a long way from Alice . . .

SIDNEY: And a long way from you . . .

REBECCA *is still not looking at* DANIEL, *not meeting his
eyes.*

SIDNEY: I have been trying to tell you, that the most
glamorous relations aren't necessarily the ones you end
up having the greatest affinity with –

DANIEL: Yes . . . (*staring over at* REBECCA.) I think you're
right, Sidney . . . (*Watching* RAYMOND *and* ESTHER.)
My parents – they seem to have found out something
about themselves . . .

(*He smiles.*) But me . . . I'm not sure how much nearer
I am, about learning who I am . . .

SIDNEY (*grins*): You're like *me* . . . that's the whole point . . .
that's why I'm here next to you . . . Determined . . . full
of hidden talents . . . and you're not going to be a
suburban surveyor for much longer . . . That's you!

DANIEL: You're a fortune teller now? . . .

SIDNEY: One doesn't have to be a genius to work that one
out . . . !

*We see all the different faces round the long table, and the
way that they've been grouped.*

DANIEL: I'm also thinking . . . (*he smiles*) about the family
tree. If family trees, if they –

SIDNEY: Wouldn't it be great if instead of being arranged
strictly by birth lines, by the conventional interpretation
of genes – they were arranged by who you shared the
most in common with?! Who you were most like in the
family?

209

DANIEL (*laughs*): Yes, that's exactly what I was thinking too. *We see the family tree, moving, shifting. The Underground map of lines, changing. We see* DANIEL*'s name pulling towards* SIDNEY, *and then towards* ALICE.

We cut back to the dinner table. ALICE *is quite close to* DANIEL *on the table. He watches her closely for a second. We cut back to the family tree, his name is getting closer and closer to* ALICE*'s.*

The moment is cut through abruptly by the sound of a glass being struck with a fork.

ERNEST Everybody . . . your attention . . . Alice has just got something to say . . .

ALICE *stands. She looks very pale. The whole table falls quiet.*

ALICE: I just want to say . . . I just . . . (*She falters for a second.*) I just want to welcome you all obviously. And to say first and foremost we're here to celebrate Martina and Thomas's engagement . . . (*There is applause.*)

MARTINA (*beams*): I am so, so happy you're all here! (*She laughs.*) And even more of you than I expected!

IRVING*'s eyes flash at this and he helps himself to more drink.*

ALICE (*she's fighting to retain her control, to remain poised*): And of course to celebrate Ernest's great hospitality too.

ERNEST *smiles vaguely, acknowledging the applause.*

ALICE: And there's going to be fantastic food, as you can already smell, I know – and dancing too, of course . . . and a chance . . . to explore the grounds at night even –

She pauses. People look up, uncertain why she has stopped. Silence.

ALICE: I just want to say *one* other thing. Because there is nothing so bad as people making big speeches *before* the food, maybe big speeches at any time . . . But . . . (*She stops. She looks down the table, at all of them.*) What I want

210

to say is – some of you will remember this house, some of you may have been here as children . . . And also there are many of you here who attended the reunion, who have come face to face with memories . . . Some good, obviously, some maybe less happy . . .

So I would just like to propose we drink to those who are no longer with us . . . those who couldn't be here . . .

We will all have our own private list, of course . . . *The sound begins to cut out. We see the veiled face of* HENRIETTA, *and then we see intense close-ups of* DANIEL's GRANDFATHER *and* HENRIETTA *together, and then the faces of* VIOLET *and* EDITH *as they are now round the table, thinking about their younger selves, and immediately after, the two little girls walking and walking, and their wild faces staring through the foliage of the wood.* GRACE *sitting looking ahead, severely, and then as her glorious younger self.* STEPHEN *and then his mother, the little girl running down the long staircase in Nazi Germany. And we see a close-up of* REBECCA *remembering her younger self staring with rapt attention at* ALICE, *as she tells her a story. We cut back to* REBECCA, *the sense of loss in her face. Then we cut to* ALICE.

ALICE: I would like above all to mention my friend Richard, who I loved as a child . . . *as my own child* . . . (*her voice falters*) and who is not with us any more . . .
REBECCA *looks up at* ALICE, *she's surprised.* CHARLES *watches* ALICE. ALICE *finishes with great dignity.*

ALICE (*raising her glass*): To all of us . . . and to a great night . . . Thank you.
We see people clapping and drinking round the table. DANIEL *and* ALICE's *eyes meet.* CHARLES, *way down the table from* ALICE, *toasts her with his glass. Then we see* REBECCA, *her look has softened, she's moved by this public recognition of* RICHARD's *life. The sound cuts out.* ALICE

211

resumes her seat, sitting poised and quiet, as people are
laughing and talking all around her.

IRVING: Photo! Photo! The family . . . !

    IRVING *is shouting, he has jumped up with a camera and he*
is standing on a chair. Everybody looks up at him. He takes
a photo with a flash.

    The picture of the family fills the screen, they're all looking
up at the camera, and then it melts to black.

Credits.